OXPECKER

Poetry for Picky Eaters

M.C. THEDIECK

Oxpecker Press

Deland, FL

ISBN: 979-8-9903830-0-5 (hardcover)
ISBN: 979-8-9903830-3-6 (paperback)
ISBN: 979-8-9903830-1-2 (e-book)
ISBN: 979-8-9903830-2-9 (audiobook)

Library of Congress Control Number: 2024910840

Edited by Charlotte Meares
Interior illustrations by Hailey MacIsaac
Cover and interior design by Jess LaGreca, Mayfly book design

First printing edition 2024

Oxpecker Press
Deland, FL
oxpeckerpress.com

To my parents, who exposed me to the arts
and took me to hear poets read their works
(at least a little culture sunk in),
and to Marylese for her patience
and encouragement.
See? I was listening.

CONTENTS

UMAMI

Proem Poe-M

Through the deepest, darkest times, I write—with no intent to be Poe-ish (though we two showed up at the Battle of Black Bile during the War of Melancholia!)—to drain the blackness from my being. My mate of some twenty-odd (perhaps odder to me that she is still by my side) years has seen me through interesting times—from bleakest to brightest. Her secret is a rather cagey strategy. She supports my decision to escape to whatever there is or isn't on the other side, but only after I've reached the fourteenth day. If, on the fourteenth day, I still needed "to do it"—however "it" needed to be done—so be it.

Sometime around 2012, an abyss opened. For the next three years, she hung on to me as I dangled, suspended between her world and an often too-beckoning depth. On waking, upon trying to sleep, I counted days. Five. Seven. Nine. Twelve. Once, I reached thirteen. But never fourteen. Or this little book of poetry would have been a posthumous testament to my failure to keep holding her heroic hand. Gradually, the darkness melted into light. Sometimes, I slip too close to the edge of that chasm, even imagine that I'm suspended over melancholy's gaping maw. But I do not let go. Instead, I write. For me. For her. For you.

—M. C. Thedieck

SWEET

I Believe

I believe in everything and nothing in equal measure.
I believe in the sun's rays because I trust physics,
and I believe in moonbeams because I trust my heart.
I believe in the power of medicine to heal the body,
and in the power of hope to raise the spirit.
I believe a child's hug is strong enough
to bring a grown man to his knees,
and a dog's lick on his face is strong enough
to raise him back off the floor.
I believe in the vastness of the universe.
I believe in the intimacy of holding hands.
I believe that no smile will ever go unnoticed, even by the blind.
I believe that we are born complete, no additives needed,
except our need for love,
love is the perfect medium in which to grow.
I believe that all we can be isn't predetermined,
yet it's never really in doubt.
I believe that given enough love,
unconditional love,
we are enough.

The Accident

It was an accident
A slip
A mishandling
It only hurt for a second
Then it was just numb
And dripping

I should have run to the bathroom
Or at least put pressure on it
But I didn't
The flow fascinated me
And I was numb

I kept thinking how little it hurt
And how easily it flowed
And how numb I felt
And how easy the next one was
And how rhythmic it all seemed

It was inconsiderate of me
Such a mess
But I was numb
And the aggregate was so rich
And viscous

I sat on the kitchen floor
Mesmerized by the growing pool
My hands could not leave it alone
Fingers painting like those of a child
I smeared a quick apology
Then ran out

Cat's Spring

Spring
has taken the chill
out of the air,
and the cat has
been booted back
outside
to sink or swim
in his own milieu.

Which is just fine with him.

Afterlife of the Party

I would very much like for there to be an afterlife.
But in my version, there would be no eternity,
just a party,
like a very big cast party,
where everyone and everything
that you encountered
in your life are there
not to berate you,
but just to tell you your life's impact
from their perspective.
Every ant, every tree, every bird, and frog,
and everything you ever touched or saw
is there to give you their side of things.
It's all very amicable,
Cocktails beforehand,
a cornucopia of gourmet food
served as a seven-course meal.
Lots of laughter and good conversation.
You get to see and hear—
from a different point of view—
from all the players, large and small,
just what your life was all about.
And after the wine is gone,
and the food eaten,
and the last entity has left,
you cross the room to the exit,
put your hand on the light switch,
take a very deep breath,
let it out with a long sigh,
and turn out the lights.
Poof.

You
and all the rest
are simply
gone.
A lifetime flashed
before the light
flickered out.

Stillness

Summer is on high
and so too is the heat.
It's not just the heat that oppresses;
it's the humidity—
the thickness of the air,
heavy, wet, still.

If the humidity is high enough,
prolonged exposure will inhibit your
ability to sweat.
Makes it a struggle to even draw a breath.
We must all be part fish.
It feels like,
if you closed your eyes
and really concentrated,
you could swim up into the sky,
to the tops of the trees,
where the leaves are motionless.

Everything is stilled by the density.
Blades of grass,
petals on the gardenia blooms.
Even the sweet smell of the jasmine
is constricted,
hanging in layers,
less permeating,
more like
rivers of fragrance
in an ocean of thick,
viscous air.

Grief

Grieving
is a lonely process.
There is no right or wrong way to grieve.
No shortcut for getting through it.
Recognize those times you had
together and apart
(although too short by any measure)
were
cherished times.
Remember the good times.
Remember the not-so-good times.
But remember that person,
as a whole
healthy
happy
human being
whom you were privileged to know,
to share love with,
to be a part of.
And try to understand
that what they would most likely want
is for you to
hold them ever so close to your heart,
forever,
and let them go.

When Clouds Descend

Good friend,
his Jeep CJ-5,
a handle of Wild Turkey,
and a little Mother Earth herb.

He knows all the back roads in North Georgia.
And he knows most of the trails.
He finds this logging cut
that takes us to the top of the world.

We roll to the middle of the clearing
and shut the engine off.
We dispense the herb
and wash it down with the Turkey.

Facing west,
we watch as the sun
scrolls down the last hour of the day.
The twilight is spectacular.

The conversation that had
been flowing lazily all day
fades to silent reverence as we
watch the world slowly go dark.

The deer come out,
slowly approach the Jeep,
nearly pressing their noses against the windows
and ask: "You boys OK?"

Judging us benign,
they return to their grazing,
and we gather ourselves
for the return down the cut.

Rutted and washed-out track.
His little mule struggles
to keep her footing.
Then, we're enveloped by the mist.

Our attention, enraptured by the sunset,
failed to notice that the clouds had gone down, too.
Now we're in thick soup
and can't see three feet in front of us.

With no clear landmarks,
vision and decisions slightly impaired,
our homeward traverse slows to a crawl,
with a lot of guessing.

Left here or right there?
Straight here or left there?
How many cuts, trails, and tracks are there
in these ancient woods?

I'm no help in navigation,
being on foreign soil.
Words of encouragement
are all I have to offer.

Finally, his surefooted mule
rolls onto asphalt with a centerline.
Still disorientated, we sit and ponder,
left or right?

A county road must go somewhere.
Heads or tails?
Twenty minutes down the road
our headlights resolve the quandary as to our whereabouts

Seems we aren't going to be home
anytime soon,
for in our fog of fog,
we have come out on the backside of the mountain

and
are
now
in
Tennessee.

Spotlight

There is no light
hotter or brighter
than that of
self-interrogation
when done correctly.

God in the House

God dropped by our house last night.
Just showed up unannounced.
Insisted on taking us out to dinner.
"Where?" I asked.
"The Golden Corral," he said. "I love their endless salad bar."

Now, I'm not trying to make a big deal out of this,
but, what would you do if,
out of the blue, God dropped by your house,
insisted on taking you out to dinner,
and you ended up at . . . the Golden Corral?

Couldn't Mr. High and Mighty
have taken us someplace a little nicer?
It's not like he couldn't afford it
or he couldn't get us a reservation anywhere else.
Besides, me and the missus were kind of looking forward to
a nice quiet evening by ourselves. But noooo . . .
Instead, God dragged us out to the Golden Corral
because he loves their endless salad bar.

To make matters worse,
after he finished eating his "endless salad,"
he announced that he wanted to come back to our house
and play charades. Charades?
I haven't played charades since junior high,
just before I learned how to play spin the bottle.
I tried to dissuade him of this idea,
but got a swift kick in the shin from the missus
and "the look."
You know . . . *the look*!

It says everything without saying a word.
"Be nice to your friend, dear,
or you'll never get laid again as long as you live,
which, at the rate you're going,
won't be too much longer, anyway."

Soooo, I found myself sitting on my sofa,
watching God tap two fingers on his forearm and tug on his ear lobe,
trying to figure out what the hell he wanted me to guess.
The category?
Someone he knew.
Oh, now that narrowed it down.
At least they had to be living,
which was more than I could say for myself at the time.

All I could think was, "Dear God, I'm going to be at this all night."

Jitterbug

The mommas and the poppas
are jitterbugging in the tree.
They're dancing limb to limb
with their feathers flying free.

I'm sittin' on the back porch
just smokin' my cigar,
when I glimpsed that cloud a comin',
it was a comin' from afar.

That big black ball o' dots
kept on changin' shape,
swoopin' and a soarin'
like a big ol' magic cape.

Those birds made such a racket,
descending on that oak.
They covered every branch
like they was a feathered cloak.

Looking for a soul mate
or maybe just to tease,
they filled the tree with chatter
as it swayed them in the breeze.

It wasn't even dark yet,
but the Big Band's in full swing,
all warmed up and rarin' to go,
playin' "Sing, Sing, Sing."

The mommas and the poppas
are jitterbugging in the tree.
They're dancing limb to limb
with their feathers flying free.

What If

What if I was the child who died?
What if, drawn back to the place
where I think that I grew up,
I find out that I was that child.
What if all that happened,
in my mind,
was only the fleeting possibility
of my life
if I had lived?
But I hadn't.
What if I go back and see that it wasn't real?
What if I find a grave marker with my name on it,
having died at birth?
Would the fleeting moment end
and my infantile mind let go of the possibility?
Would my wife no longer exist,
or would she be married to someone else?
And what of my son?
Would he vanish without a trace,
never having been,
or would he be someone else's son?
And if I stay away from that place,
is that any guarantee
that I will complete this life to its end?
What end have I dreamed up for myself?
I shut my eyes,
take a deep breath,
and pull
the trigger.
Let's find
the answers
without the trip.

Tourist

His baggage—
each piece hand tooled
with great care,
stacked one on top of the other,
piling ever higher—
was slowly
portaging him
to
his
grave.

Pocket Watch

A little while ago, I inherited a pocket watch. This watch is an heirloom, made of gold with an inscription dated 1879. It has one hand, an hour hand. Over the years, I have acquired a collection of nice, inexpensive—meaning less than five hundred dollars—wrist watches. I purchased them as timepieces that also function as jewelry: wardrobe accessories. I'm not a ring, necklace, or bracelet kind of guy, so they were an agreeable compromise and helped to advance my style a notch.

Then I bought my first cell phone—the brick with the ten-inch antenna. Then a flip phone, a "Crackberry," emerging from the dark ages, a smartphone, followed by a "fourth-generation" smartphone, whatever that meant. All of these devices display time—down to the one-hundredth of a second—clearly on their faces. And all made the wristwatch less and less a time piece and more and more a bracelet with a watch face. Eventually, mine stayed buried in the watch box at the back of my dresser. So much for wardrobe enhancement. I'm back down to schlub status as far as my accessorizing is concerned, but I'm certainly not alone in my technology choices. That shift does present me with a problem when I'm traveling. I usually turn my smartphone off and stick it in my carry-on before boarding a plane. Call me old school, but I refuse to be a slave to the damn thing. Flying is time that I can capture and truly call my own. But then I don't know what time it is. As a result, I have become adept at taking furtive glances at other people's wrists. Those that still wear a watch, anyway.

On a recent flight, as per norm, I packed my cell phone in my carry-on and stuck that in the overhead compartment. I settled in for the one-hour flight. A delayed pushback from the gate and further delay on the tarmac had my anxiety soaring well before the plane finally took off. Concerned about making my next connection, I looked around for a wrist with a watch. The gentleman sitting next to me wore a slick-looking device that had a blank black face, inside a slick black case, strapped to his wrist with a matte black strap.

In that moment, I realized that technology—and time—had left me behind just as surely as they had left behind the first owner of my heirloom gold pocket watch with just an hour hand.

A Change in the Weather

This morning, I woke up early, earlier than normal. As I tried to gather my senses and come to some sort of reasonable conclusion as to why I was awake at this ungodly hour, I started to realize that I was cold. I had gone to sleep with just a sheet draped over me and the ceiling fan on to combat the heat. But merely five hours later, I was cold.

I got up just long enough to relieve myself, turn off the fan, retrieve a light blanket from the closet shelf, and burrow back in for a few more hours, smug in the thought that I wouldn't be interrupted by any more intrusions or annoying urges. As I drifted back into the half-zone, that area between really asleep and really awake, I thought about the weather. More specifically, the change in the weather, and a tranquility that had come with it.

Later, after the intended time to get up had come and gone, after showering and dressing, swallowing pills, brushing teeth, while walking Tai the dog, I noticed the sensation again—like the world was running at three-quarter speed.

I asked Tai if he had noticed it, too. Being the type of dog that Tai is, full Chow, red coat, black tongue, grumpy disposition, he ignored me. Instead, he chose to pick a fight with some dog across the street, two blocks away.

Tai can truly be an asshole, but I love him, and he loves me—in his Tai way. When I come home at night, I get to pet him twice, he doesn't tolerate three times. If nothing else, he is predictable. You always know where you stand with him. Usually at a safe distance.

Completely sidetracked by his clever subterfuge, I thought no more about the weather, or what effects it may be having on me and on the three-quarter speed of everything. I made my way to work, unaware of my muted surroundings or the daze that I seemed to be in.

Like my last phone conversation with you, whom I have known for a total of thirteen days (there's that number 13 again, which I'll explain some other time), including the night I met you at your boyfriend's going-away party, was more like that of a couple who have been to-gether for years and have a history. We discovered we're both scared shitless about what we're contemplating.

"Hi, how's it going? . . . Oh I'm sorry about your upset stomach . . . How are the kids? . . . How's your tan coming along? . . . I think we should do it at the judge's chambers . . . I miss you . . . Drive carefully going home . . . See you tomorrow."

So where did all the panic and fear go? And why didn't I notice? Shouldn't there be at least a little trepidation?

I get it. It's not really the world that's at three-quarter speed. It's me. Not dazed, not duped, not slow, just unhurried. Dare I say, serene?

The rest of the workday went by, well . . . not exactly unnoticed. The city had a media event for a baggage test out at the new airport, and the local press were given an exclusive in the bowels of the basement where the little cars that hold the individual bags run along a track suspended thirty feet in the air and do their magic. Boy, the system put on a show. Cars bumping into each other and jamming, luggage not ar-riving at the correct location, bags getting spit onto the track in front of a car, and the car splitting the luggage open, the contents of unrepa-triated bags falling on the observers. The fiasco made national news.

The system designers put on a somber defense at the debriefing and promised to have everything corrected in time for the next test in thirteen days. The baggage delivery system was already a full year late.

Game, set, match, day over. Drive home. Walk Tai. Talk to you again. More phone serenity. "Should we leave the furniture? What about the cars? . . . I'm glad you had enough sense to come in out of the sun before your hives set in . . . See you tomorrow." Just how numb am I?

Then a phone call to my son. "Hi . . . I love you . . . Here's Mom."

"Hello. Yes, I'll schedule the house to go on the market by the 10th . . . Write any negativity about the house on toilet paper, flush it, and release it . . . What the____? . . . I'm sorry you missed a chance at a relationship with Ross (I'm starting to get good at this) . . . I'm glad that you have managed to salvage a relationship with Paul . . . (Not) . . . Gee, that's great that you had a fun blind date . . . (OK, that may have been over the top) . . . Yes, I would like to keep a friendship with you." (I hated her for the next thirteen years. It was a waste of energy. She never went away, and I still had to see her at special occasions.)

Out to the pizza parlor. Why are pizza joints referred to as parlors?

The weather issue struck me again. It's . . . it's . . . fall! A reminder that things do change. The season is changing. It will be hot again—there's no doubt—but here it is, right here, right now, and I'm almost uncomfortable in my short-sleeved shirt.

And that damn three-quarter-speed shit. It's definitely me. I'm fluid. Almost floating. As I watch the rest of the world rush by, I'm unhurried and unaffected and calm and the weather . . . cool . . . the season . . . changed . . . and I'm tranquil . . . in the midst of total chaos, I've actually found inner peace.

I get it. I finally get it. It's so clear. Every piece fits perfectly, interlocking with those pieces already in place. Falling—as if out of the sky. A true change in the weather.

I love you. And, oh, by the way, I left the winning lotto ticket at the pizza parlor. Forgive me?

Things to Give

I stand before you,
a man of modest means,
with but few things
to offer.
Two legs,
with which to stand by you.
Two arms,
with which to hold you
and never to let you go.
Two eyes,
with which to consume your beauty.
Two ears,
with which to appropriate
your innermost thoughts.
One nose,
with which to ingest your essences.
One mouth,
with which to avow your praises
and cover you with kisses.
And one heart,
with which to love you
fiercely.
This humble humanity
I give to you freely.
My only request,
that you cherish them
as much as
I cherish
You.

Treetops

After a long
summer day,
the sun illuminates
only the very tops
of my trees.
From dawn,
it's played
with Cloud and Breeze,
dappled with Leaf and Branch,
crossed Garden and Grass,
splashing multicolored patterns and shapes,
displayed its
blue-blazing brilliance at noon,
waned,
receded into
more muted tones,
settled again
in the topmost boughs,
swaying to
Breeze's adagio,
eyes slowly closing,
letting
night
descend.

Us

You.
Me.
Hot dark night,
grunts and growls,
tight grips on loose hair,
pushing toward that spot you know,
that free fall from our high cliff,
flying through the air,
screaming and howling,
landing with familiar panting
and dripping.

Slowly we gather ourselves
in search of a new cliff
to jump off together.

Have I mentioned that I miss you?

Talkative

The wind likes to talk.
Sometimes it whispers softly in your ear.
Other times it shouts your house down.
And sometimes it fancies shooting the breeze.
It's loquacious by nature,
an incorrigible magpie.
Never tell a secret to the wind.
It broadcasts opprobrium near and far.
It treats your confidentiality like dandelion pappus.
If you can be still and listen,
sift through the detritus,
It will tell you profound truths.

SOUR

Me First

I have to go now.
I have to go first.
I haven't the strength
to witness the worst.
I haven't the courage
to follow the hearse.

A coward I am,
a sham and a lie.
a spoiled only child
who just wouldn't try,
a man in name only
who can't watch you die.

Put me inside
and bury me deep.
Just don't leave me first
for that infinite sleep,
don't leave me behind,
to languish and weep.

Clean off your hands
from tamping the earth.
Shed that last tear
for hiding your mirth.
You make me proud.
I haven't the worth.

Six Drops

Six drops.
That's all we got.
Six drops
can't even be counted
as rain.
You could almost hear the plants
stretch and strain to catch them.
It's so dry.
Each day
the weatherman
gives us false hope of rain.
Yet nothing comes of it.
Most days,
the clouds don't even come.
And when they do,
they just hold tight
and pass us by.
Our drops came from such wisps
that gave their everything.
But just six drops were all they had.

Down

Down
I'm down

Down for the count
Down and out
Down at the heel
Down in the mouth
Down in the dumps

Just down

Down the road
Down on my luck
Down on all fours
Down the crapper
Down and dirty

Just down

Downsized
Downtrodden
Downcast
Downhearted

Through man.

I'M DOWN!

Just. Down.

Repetition

The impact sprinkler,
pulsating jets
of water
in circles
across the lawn:
tik . . . tik . . . tik
shhh . . . shhh . . . shhh
its amaranthine motion,
keeping time,
counting seconds,
with such gravity,
like the metronome
and the pendulum.

The sun
turning a tree
from black
silhouette,
to gold,
to brilliant green,
as it arcs
across the sky,
only to turn
back to gold
then black silhouette
once again.

The cycle
of the seasons
of mistakes,
having only
different names.
The follies
of life forms.
Time,
days aggregate
into weeks,
then flow
into months
and run into years.

If only
I could
turn time off
as easily
as the hose.
Drip, drip, drip . . .
Life is
a fractal pattern
of germinate
and flourish,
wilt and wither,
dwindle
and die.

For me,
however,
there is no
cycle of samsara.
For on
this stage
two things
I will not repeat:
the opening act
and the
last scene.
Curtain closed.
No encores.

tik . . . tik . . . tik
shhh . . . shhh . . . shhh

V Is for

Roses are red,
violets are blue,
I went out to buy
a valentine for you.

Most were too sappy,
some were just wrong,
a few looked promising,
but never that strong.

So onward my quest
down the next row
to read more cards
that I hoped would show

How much I still love you,
how much I still care
that you are my everything
Blah, blah, blah . . . OK, I give . . .

I didn't look for a card.
I should have, I'm sorry.
But do I get any credit
for a sappy poem?

Transient

Transient: lasting only for a short time; impermanent.

I have always felt transient,
impermanent,
not belonging,
just passing through.
I'm meant to be somewhere else.
It's an odd feeling.
You just start a new job,
and yet you feel you aren't
in the right place at the right time.
When I was younger,
I was sure that I wouldn't make it to thirty.
Yet, now that I'm more than twice that age,
I still feel that I should be
on the next train out of here.
My bags seem to be perpetually packed.
It's very disquieting.
I expect something to happen
that will disrupt everything
and plant me in
more suitable soil.
Somewhere I can grow roots.
Someplace that nurtures my soul
and calms my being,
so that I'm not so
transient.

Isles

Islands.
Islands in the stream.
Stream of consciousness.
Conscious not to hurt.

Too late.
The damage done.
I don't know what I did.
I don't know how deep the wound.

I only know
I never meant to hurt
You,
Me,
Islands.

Streams apart.

Gremlins

Victor Orlanzo was introduced to me through a friend of a friend. In my business as a specialty contractor, word of mouth is crucial for continued success. My niche requires cultivating clients carefully. Getting that first job is the hardest. From then on, I just have to do good work for a reasonable price and, at the end of the day, make the client happy.

Sometimes that means giving a little bit back at the end of a project. You know how that goes. You still make your profit, just maybe not as much as you thought you would.

Stella hates that part. Stella, a chain smoker with a raspy voice who doesn't take any guff from anybody, runs the office, keeps the books, and basically keeps me afloat. At every moment, she knows where every dime is coming from or going to. She also has a way with the crew. She treats each one completely different, yet they all think that she treats them exactly the same. Now that's a talent.

My painter is a true artist, or "artiste," as she likes to say. Arabella, Ari as we call her, was classically trained. She went to school, then studied under a master for a number of years. Unfortunately, that master was running a forgery ring. When the feds set up a sting, Ari got caught up in the bust and did some time. When she got out, the only work she could get was commercial drudgery. She hated it.

I caught wind of her though friends and hired her as my muralist. Her art is phenomenal. Every client practically weeps over her work. She's a perfectionist, will drive you crazy, a bit of a diva, and an incorrigible flirt, but at the end of a project, she's worth her weight in gold. It doesn't hurt that she's drop-dead gorgeous.

Dwayne and Bobby are my carpenters. They seem to be joined at the hip. You never see one without the other. I don't think they have a ninth-grade education between them. But come time to make sawdust, they're every bit the artists that Ari is. Their medium just happens to be wood, not paint. Neither weighs 150 lbs. soaking wet.

Then there's Duda. None of us know what Duda's real name is. Not even Stella. He gets paid in cash. We don't ask, and he doesn't tell. Duda is a master electrician and plumber. He's also a very large Black man with a permanent scowl. Duda wires all of the fountains and fancy lighting. He can synchronize them to amazing effects. Dwayne and Bobby think that he was in one of the unions up north somewhere, got sideways with the mob and fell—or was pushed—off the grid.

My job is to keep the wheels rolling. Make sure that Ari has her paints, D & B have their work laid out in front of them, and nobody messes with Duda. Our niche is finishing interiors of fancy restaurants.

We come in as a sub-contractor to the general contractor, or we're hired directly by the owner. For this job, Mr. Orlanzo hired us directly. The GC on this project was a big-name, hardball group that didn't like us not being under their control—or their profit margin. Their superintendent on the project was an OK guy named Stan.

Stan had come up through the trades, made super before he was thirty, and never progressed beyond that. He's now in his early sixties. Some people are born superintendents: being in an office would just get under their skin. Stan is one of those. Capable, competent, come in, get the job done, and move on to the next one. But I wouldn't classify Stan as a company man.

Mr. Orlanzo's project was Stan's first with this GC, and he definitely didn't like the project manager. Phil was one of those PMs who thought that the project couldn't run without him. He'd come out to the job site once a week, stand in the middle of it, arms folded, hardhat all bright and shiny, chinos creased and pressed, oxford button-down freshly starched and ironed from the cleaners, and tell everyone how they were doing it wrong. Stan would stand behind him, rolling his eyes, trying to make sure that something didn't fall on Phil.

If you aren't the superintendent, then yelling at the troops is a real bad idea on a construction site. It cuts the legs out from under the super and un-motivates everyone in general. If someone needs yellin' at on a site, the super better be the one doing it, and if he's any good, there won't be much yellin' or chewin'. Good supers know when to push, when to pull, and when to chew. And Stan was a good one. Still, every time Phil would come out to the site, he would undo pretty much everything Stan had done the whole week before. Then Stan would have to spend all of next week fixing it, only to have Phil show up and undo it all again.

Stan had brought the project along at a good pace and was on schedule, despite Phil's "input." We came in once the structure was up and started doing our thing. Phil had a special hatred for my crew. He would nitpick everything, and for some reason, my guys were f—ing up by the numbers on this one, which didn't help the situation. D & B installed the trim upside down. Ari painted murals on the wrong walls. Duda had leaks, sparks, and shorts everywhere. In short, it was a mess.

Periodically, Mr. Orlanzo would come out to look at the progress, and Phil would trail him like a puppy. If Mr. Orlanzo would have stopped short, Phil would have broken his nose on Mr. Orlanzo's butt. Phil took great delight in pointing out each and every flaw in our work. Mr. Orlanzo would look at it and nod, look at me, raise an eyebrow, and I would tell him that it would be fixed, on time. He would nod again and walk on.

This sent Phil into silent rages. He would turn beet red and you could almost see the steam coming out of his ears. Phil was sure that he could get us run off of the project; so sure, in fact, that he had gone so far as to hire a second crew and had them sit outside in their trucks for a week, waiting for Mr. Orlanzo to fire us. But Mr. Orlanzo never did, and Phil had to pay for their time and send them home.

The job was getting down to crunch time, and Stan had his work well under control. My work, on the other hand, was not cooperating, so we were the only crew working well into the night the last two weeks before turnover. Much to everyone's amazement, we staggered to the finish line on time.

The following week, Mr. Orlanzo was having a friends-and-family shakedown dinner to get the restaurant ready for the grand opening the next week. He invited my group as part of the construction team. Phil was there—expensive suit, trophy wife in tow—holding court with anyone he could corner, telling them how he single-handily brought the project in on time.

Stan was there, sitting at the bar by himself, nursing a bourbon on the rocks. I settled on the barstool to his right and asked what was next for him. He stared straight ahead for a few moments.

"I'm thinking of retiring," he said. "This might be a good one to go out on."

I wanted to pursue it, but Stella came up and whispered in my ear. Seemed we had a bit of a problem brewing in the men's room that called for my imitate attention. Patting Stan on the shoulder, I went to see what needed doing. When I pushed on the men's room door, it seemed blocked by something. I leaned in enough to push the object out of the way and slip inside. The "object" was Dwayne, passed out cold on the floor. Bobby was standing—or should I say, weaving—over him, about ready to go down himself.

Stella followed me in, took a quick look at the situation, spun on her heels, and headed out of the room to find Duda. In the time it took Stella to bring Duda to the men's room, I had dumped enough cold water on Dwayne to get him conscious and had propped Bobby up against the wall. Duda and I got Dwayne on his feet. With Dwayne tucked under Duda's left arm and Bobby under his right, the men looked like rag dolls.

Stella led the way out to the back of the van where Duda deposited the guys like two sacks of potatoes. I watched them drive off to pour coffee into those two knuckleheads and went back inside. Ari was in one of her "masterpiece" rooms, conducting a tour of her work as if this were an art gallery opening. She gave me one of her patented evil looks, threw her nose in the air, and continued her lecture on fine art. I thought about how she could be both charming and spellbinding, when she wanted to be.

Phil was holding Mr. Orlanzo captive by the kitchen door. I could tell by the way Mr. Orlanzo kept looking at his watch that he was getting antsy. He spotted me across the dining area and raised his eyebrow. I nodded back and tapped my watch.

Stan was still sitting at the bar with his Bourbon.

"Let's go outside and have a smoke," I said, motioning with my head.

He looked at me kind of funny. He had never seen me smoke on the job. In fact, he knew that I didn't. He thought about it for a second, downed his drink, and gave me a Stan-like "Sure." A short ways down the sidewalk, I pulled out a lighter and lit his cigarette. He leaned in, got his cigarette going, took a deep drag, held it for a moment, and slowly, deliberately, pushed the smoke through his nostrils.

"So, what's up?" he finally asked.

"Stan, you're a good superintendent," I said, making sure we made eye contact. "You know how to run a project, and you know how not to let the brass upset the applecart. If you want to continue to work, but under a little less stress, then give me a call."

I handed him my business card and an envelope. He looked at it for a moment and wordlessly put it in his pocket.

"It's time for you to go home, Stan."

He looked at me squarely, straightened up just a little, took one last drag on his cigarette, dropped it on the sidewalk, and crushed it with his big boot. With a slight nod, he walked away.

Back inside once again, I got halfway across the main dining area when black smoke started billowing out of the kitchen. The head chef burst out the doors yelling, "Fire!"

Calmly, I pulled the fire alarm. The place quickly went into full panic mode. Everyone rushed for the exits. Ari was one of those hurrying past me, and as she did, she gave me a dirty look. I made sure no one was left in the building, then headed to the parking lot.

The fire department was handicapped by a cascade of issues. First, the fire alarm never rang through to the monitoring company, so the fire department wasn't immediately notified. By the time the fire department arrived, the building was fully engulfed. The sprinkler system never deployed. When the pump truck showed up and charged the system through the fire department connection, no water came out of the sprinkler heads. The pressure at the site fire hydrant was low. The building burned to the ground, and all the fire department could do was keep the blaze from spreading to nearby structures.

A few hours later, Mr. Orlanzo found me at the far end of the parking lot.

What was left of the building crackled and hissed. Over to the side, the Fire Chief and a police lieutenant were having a little chat with Phil. He no longer looked like he was in control of the situation.

Mr. Orlanzo reached into his breast pocket and handed me my final check and a rather thick envelope.

"I really appreciate the work you did," he said. "Your crew was everything you said they would be. I thought your price was a little high, but I'm happy that I got more than I paid for."

Stella pulled up with the van. I climbed in the front passenger seat, rolled down the window, and leaned out as she started to drive off.

"Victor, gremlins are expensive."

Victor Orlanzo grinned and nodded as we pulled out of the parking lot and drove off into what was left of the night.

TICK Tock

There is a clock
that sits on my desk.
First it goes TICK,
and then it goes tock,
Louder on the upbeat
Quieter on the down
Like a rocking chair sounds different
forward to back,
synchronic
yet disjointed,
rock forward . . . TICK,
rock back . . . tock.
Symbiotic,
one motion incomplete without the other,
creating character and purpose.
Not just a chronometer,
but a keeper of the time.
TICK . . . tock
TICK . . . tock
TICK . . . tock

Loving You

I am not nearly as worried about losing my parents
as I am about losing you.

My life will undoubtedly wobble to a certain extent
when one or the other of them passes.
Even so, I'm sure I'll cope
and continue.

But if I were to lose you,
then *all* would be lost.
All movement would cease.
My heart would stop beating.
Though I would still live,
I would not call life viable.

Floundering evokes manageability.
No, such an experience would be
catastrophic.
Others would find me
collapsed,
shattered,
broken.

Coping would be untenable,
an impossibility.
I could not try.

My world is your world.
Each day, your tide casts me out,
and each night, I wash back up on your sacred shore.

My breath is drawn from your being.
I live because you live.
Please don't ever leave me.

Idol Gossip

For forty years, I had lost you.
I had been worshiping a ghost,
holding myself up to the faint light of a memory.

I grew up. I grew old. I grew wise.
I learned to hold myself accountable,
rely on foundations built by me, for me,
through love, nurturing, experimentation, and experience.

Yet I still wondered about you.
What had become?
Where did the facts lie,
for a while receiving only snippets of gossip,
a remnant image, a blanket of the unknown.
News stopped altogether.

Time pulled us forward.
Kids came, wives went, jobs changed.
Life wound itself around me,
and I focused on making it through.

One day, a time capsule appeared.
I, wide-eyed in wonder,
marveled at these images:
of me,
of my "Once was,"
of "Who were they?"
I think I knew them
in a past life,
memories captured with a shaky,
in the middle-of-it hand.

Thoughts raced: wants, needs, curiosities,
and the desire to fill in the blanks.

Stubbornly, I held at bay the temptation
of this information invasion
until I could no longer resist such useful tools.
I cast out my line and dropped it into the dark pool,
hooking the seemingly lost.
I landed you on the shores of now.
During our discourse we reminisced
about the one we cannot rejoin.
Unable to speak directly to him,
we communed fondly with his spirit.

Why I Want There to Be a God
(My politically incorrect rant from on high)

I truly want there to be a god.
I want an All-Presence to come down from some lofty palace
and knock some sense into humans.
I want God to remind humans, in no uncertain terms,
that they're not the most important thing on this planet.

I want God to explain that humans are
but one small part in the overall workings
of our Earthly home,
that they need to respect not only each other
but also every other creature on this planet
because we rely on all of them,
not just on some of them, or only on ourselves.

I don't exclude myself.
I'm human, too, nobody special.
Most of us need to get it through our thick skulls
that we're not the only Creation that God loves;
we humans are just one of eight million species
that God created with equal amounts of Care and Love.

I desperately want there to be a god
so that an all-powerful presence can come in
and reclaim that rightful place as Creator,
as Enabler, as Arbiter, as Authority
and save all of God's creations
that we're killing off,
either through willful acts of murder,
over-harvesting, greed, negligence,
or that we're simply elbowing out of our way.

I want God to come down from wherever
and take away all of our toys
and get us to take time out,
to put us on equal footing
with all of God's other creatures,
a part of the food chain.

Take away humanunkind's guns,
knives, spears, and sticks,
and let us face the lion
that we hunted almost into extinction
with high-powered rifles
from two hundred yards,
calling it sport.
Maybe we need to fight the lion
with our bare hands,
smell the lion's breath
as we grasp the beast's fur
in a struggle to kill or be eaten.
Let us swim with the right and bowhead whales
that we murdered and rendered into oil
so that we could light lamps when darkness fell.
Let us sleep under the stars with the wild things,
as the wild thing we once were.

I need God to explain
that this was our position
and will be again until we understand
the symbiotic relationship we had
with all of Creation—we whose
role in the big picture was to be good stewards.

I need God to help us understand
that as our kind grew,
so did our awesome responsibilities.
God needs to explain, once again,
that we were entrusted with all Creation,
entrusted with its safe keeping.
Our Earth is not to be pillaged
like some disposable, cheap toy.

God needs to remind us that Earth
was the Almighty's Gift of Creation
to be shared by all equally,
not plundered and exploited by a few.

But there is no God.
The proof is plain.
We read of it every day.
We're confronted with our disregard
for our own kind,
our disregard for all of nature
on which our lives depend.

For if there were a god,
how could that Entity sit idly by
and watch as we have become
murderers, gluttons, devourers of resources,
petty tyrants, powerbrokers, pompous
and deceived owners of the unownable?
Would a god permit our outsized egos
to proclaim ourselves the chosen species,
some of us superior to others of our kind?

How can there be a god
who would allow any part of Creation to believe
itself better than all others,
such that we, alone, claim the right
to choose who lives, who dies,
who eats, who starves,
who thrives, and who struggles.

There cannot be a god,
if for no other reason than an All-Knowing Creator
would not permit humans to usurp divine authority,
to replace the will of an Almighty with their own,
and to do it all in the Divine's name.

Or would God?

Or Not

I'm getting ready to have a heart attack.
Or I think that I am.
Or maybe not.
That's the problem with being
a hypochondriac.
I can talk myself into and out of
almost anything.
It's really just a back pain,
a pinched nerve
that's causing this chest discomfort.
Or not.
My arm doesn't hurt.
Isn't that one sure sign?
I shouldn't be able to exercise vigorously
for 40 minutes and not be
completely winded,
should I?
Or not.
But my exercise was fine.
No pain at all.
Yet, now my chest hurts.
It's probably nothing.
Or not.

Time Change

The longer I live and the older I get,
the more I become the antichrist of change.
The NOMW of nimbleness,
I want permanence.
I want things to remain recognizable,
and repeatable.
I woke up this morning and
thought about not changing my wristwatch
back to standard time from daylight savings.
But my watch had changed itself.
It's connected to my smartphone,
which, in turn, is connected to a satellite,
which, in turn, is connected to the internet,
which has become the quintessence of change,
which in turn connects me to
a ubiquitous, seething flux,
which I hate.
I'm going back to bed!

Redheads

Redheads,
wild and dangerous creatures,
exuberant with sensual appeal,
intoxicants that enrapture,
became my Achilles' heel.

First Red
with whom my addiction started,
burned through all the phases,
mellowed to a friendship,
never really parted.

Big Red,
a temptress and a tease,
gave me what I deserved:
my waxen wings melted,
juice not worth the squeeze.

Momma Red
an older woman's desire,
A young man's dream,
never came to fruition,
a fated couple's quagmire.

Soft Red
Victorian with demurity.
voluptuous, yet refined,
desires torrid beneath the surface,
still, I acceded to her purity.

Final Red
I've made my peace,
no longer chasing,
flames of misplaced passion
happily sated by my Miss Marylese.

The Reaper's Train
(Ode to a Cockatiel)

I listen to the ticking clock
meter my time in tranquility.
The dog snores softly 'neath the covers.
A wine glass, playing in thin air, hovers,
and the Reaper's train thrums and beckons to me.

Black as night itself,
invisible to nearly all who yet draw a breath,
coupled engines shoulder the strain
of the burden borne by Reaper's train,
hauling souls leaving life for death.

Conductor, hand upon the red-hot throttle,
adjudicating which souls to take and which to keep.
This night, I am sure to feel his scythe,
then tossed inside his train to writhe
somewhere between my mortal self and final sleep.

Invading my room in stone cold stealth,
with one swift move, he's atop my chest.
His crushing weight has pinned me as his prey.
On bent knees close, he makes his grim assay.
A bony finger protruding from cloak sleeve waggles.

For now is not my time.
My soul tonight, too healthy for his reaping.
Leaping away, he spirits out the opaque room.
Gasping, up I spring, released by his abysmal gloom,
Counted among the earthly, thankful to be alive.

But who do I espy, perched upon the psychopomp's shoulder?
T'was Lucky's soul, the one he claimed tonight.
Shepherd him well, O' Death, to his eternal roost.
Lead engine mounting, throttles thrusted to full boost.
The Reaper's train rolls out into the blackened night.

219

Today was so placid.
What few clouds there were
just seemed to wander
aimlessly in the blue
like large white balls
floating on the ocean,
boxing their compasses
in anticipation of
a future passage.

Later,
the sea breeze
filled in,
giving purpose,
setting a course of 219,
and south, southwest they went.

Time

I resent how time drags me along.
Why did I have to leave the summer of '67,
when playing baseball
and hanging out at the pool was my only care?
Or, even better, that winter of '78?
Her legs were so very long,
tan, and athletic.

Why bother to drag me into next week
and thrust me into that meeting
with that impossible client
who can barely veil
his wish to see me dead
and whom I need to make happy
in order to keep my job?

Why can't I just spend the rest of my time
in a Groundhog Day kind of limbo,
a continual replay of last weekend,
lazily enjoying Friday night,
Saturday, and Sunday,
using each repeat to perfect the experience?

Or, maybe, I can just pull
the covers over my head
until the world just goes away.
God, I hate Mondays!

BooBoo, Lost

This weekend, we lost BooBoo, although "lost" is a strange word for euthanize. We didn't lose her (for Christ's sake); we dug the hole. We know right where we put her. She'll never be lost again. She had Cushing's disease, and we had been treating it for some time. My wife was constantly preparing me for the loss—or to put it more bluntly—telling me to get myself prepared because she was sure that I would not handle BooBoo's death well. She was right about that.

But thanks to her continued disaster preparation drills, I'm doing OK. It feels like I'm standing in rough surf and random rogue waves of emotion overcome me. I don't need drugs or an intervention to get through this loss. I will simply be tossed about for a while.

What has made the loss so hard for me to deal with is that BooBoo was not a dog. She was a three-year-old "little girl," our three-year-old "daughter." You know, Mary Janes, pinafore, and all. Well, figuratively. It's bad enough to lose a beloved family pet. It's a whole other thing to lose a small child.

She came to us circuitously. An abandoned, motherless puppy, she had been living on the streets for a while when a friend's son found her and took her in. But the young man didn't have time for her and passed her along to his mother. It seemed no one could offer her a permanent home.

That's where we came in. The puppy came with a crate, a blanket, a large amount of separation anxiety issues, and the name Kirin, like the beer. We figured that she had been through enough changes in her life, so we kept the name . . . for a while. For the first year or so, Kirin followed my wife from room to room, like her shadow.

When my wife went out into the yard to work, Kirin held on to the hem of my wife's shorts with her teeth. The only time she wasn't holding on to my wife's shorts was when she was digging holes. She would dig fast, furious, and deep, then stick her nose all the way down to the bottom of the hole and sit there, like she was smelling something. The shadow routine was bad enough, but the shorts-holding was particularly annoying. Over time, Kirin grew less and less anxious; she was still a shadow, just not as clingy.

We made the mistake of leaving Kirin home alone one evening shortly after we got her. When we returned, Kirin had chewed off the corners of our good leather sofa's back pillows. Lesson learned. We started off with her staying in her crate in the spare bedroom at night. One morning, when my wife went to let Kirin out, she called for me.

I looked up just in time to see Kirin come hopping around the corner on three legs, her head and one paw poking through a hole in her blanket. We thought it was hysterical, but Kirin didn't see any humor in it and let us know. The incident prompted moving her from the spare bedroom to our bedroom, and we purchased a crib mattress for the crate so she'd be more comfortable.

That arrangement lasted two weeks before she was fully ensconced under the sheets at the bottom of our bed. Along with her new sleeping arrangement came rituals and games. These were our feeble attempt to wear her out before bedtime. Kirin was a mixed breed. Best as any of the vets could determine, she was half American Staffordshire Terrier—AmStaff for short—and half Basenji. Her coloring and sweet face, big brown doe eyes, and large, erect pointy ears (although her head was a little squarer) were all Basenji, as was her tail, just not as tightly curled. All forty-five pounds of her solid muscle that could jump higher than six feet was AmStaff. My wife ended up with a black eye during one of those jump-on-and-off-the-bed games. Their heads collided, and my wife got the worst of it.

Two days later, when her shiner was at its black, purple, and green peak, we were grocery shopping. One woman, glaring at me intently, followed us throughout the store and into the checkout line. I thought she was going to have me arrested for spousal abuse before we could get out of there.

When we got Kirin, she had been on a strict diet that kept her fit. She was very muscular, but you could count every rib. In our indulgent world, that would never do. We increased her intake. Kirin got bigger, not fatter. Think middle linebacker, lighting quick, with an extra five pounds of muscle. Like having a forty-five-pound bowling ball running around the back yard.

Every so often she went on zoomies. She got this wide-eyed, half crazed look, ears pinned back, frozen in place, trembling with tension, poised like a rattlesnake ready to strike. Suddenly, she'd bolt and race around the yard, randomly changing direction. Looping back toward us, she would leap at our head, trying to nip our ears, then tear off again, looping back around for another pass.

Most annoying. But we could see the delight she got from it all. No doubt, she was laughing hysterically at us while we yelled at her to stop. What great sport.

About that time, we started to call her BooBoo. We had become the "House of Boogers." You know: "You little booger, you. Why did you do that?" Booger got distilled down to BooBoo, and it stuck. We joked that booboo was also slang for a serious error, but we never told her that. She wouldn't have seen the humor.

BooBoo had never been socialized as a puppy. We didn't help the situation. She was territorial. If she could see it, she owned it. She bit every dog that strayed into her yard, and she went after every dog we encountered on our walks. Once, we took her off leash at the neighborhood park, naïvely thinking that she wouldn't go outside the hedges after anyone. Wrong. BooBoo somehow caught sight of a lady and her black lab strolling down the sidewalk.

BooBoo seemed to have a special dislike for black dogs. She bolted past our grasp, through the hedges, and confronted the lab before we could intervene.

The woman called animal control and swore that BooBoo had bitten her dog. Animal control ticketed us, even though witnesses all agreed BooBoo had not bitten her lab. It was a warning. Another ticket could spell doom for BooBoo.

BooBoo's booboo, along with our own interactions with a scary and hateful neighbor, prompted us to search for a home in the country. We found two acres on a dead-end street with good neighbors. We installed an invisible fence to keep trouble at bay.

A few years later, my wife's sharp-bladed spade having chopped the invisible fence wire a few times, coupled with BooBoo's dislike of the shock collar, meant she was running around collarless and undeterred. Early on, the few times that she had gotten nicked by the fence seemed to have made an impression on her, and, for the most part, she shied away from the boundaries. For the most part.

Otherwise, BooBoo was a very sweet dog. She loved people: thought that everyone who came to the door did so just to see her. Not what you'd call a great watch dog. She still didn't like to be left alone. When we planned to leave for any length of time, we would tell her that we were going out and she had to "hold down the fort." That was her signal to bury herself as deeply as possible in our bed and sleep until we returned. She was a very heavy sleeper.

On returning, we would be unloading groceries in the kitchen before we heard her weak, feeble bark from the bedroom. That was BooBoo's warning: "There's a big, bad, ferocious dog in here. You'd better go away." One of us would go into the bedroom and find her all hunkered down on one of our pillows. Her sleepy, sheepish face, scrunched up eyes, and waggy tail told us that she was very happy we weren't burglars.

One night, BooBoo and I were sitting in the back room watching TV when we both heard a strange noise coming from the kitchen. She sat up and looked seriously toward the noise, looked worriedly at me, and then looked back toward the kitchen. I told her she needed to go see what that noise was. Eyes wide, ears alert, she looked toward the kitchen again, turned to face me. Eyes now narrowed and ears pulled back, she nudged my elbow with her muzzle. The message was clear: "No, you need to go see what it was."

As she got older, we noticed changes—physical and behavioral. Her vet was fairly sure that BooBoo had Cushing's disease. A tumor on the pituitary gland or simply an enlargement of the gland causes excess cortisone levels in the blood. Metabolism gets disrupted, leading to gastrointestinal disorders and hypertension. She was displaying all the physical signs, including massive muscle loss, swayed back, and a distended belly. None of us saw the point of expensive testing to confirm the diagnosis.

The gastrointestinal issues made her stomach hurt, which prompted her to want food. We reduced the amount of food she got per meal and added meals: 7 a.m., 10 a.m., noon, 3 p.m., 6 p.m., and the last meal at about 9 p.m.

She taught me which meal was the most important of the day: the next one.

She learned to tell time. Five minutes before the next meal, she sat in front of us, waiting for us to move. If we didn't head for the kitchen in what she thought was an appropriate amount of time, she barked. It was never vicious or aggressive, just persistent, and annoying. She tilted her head up, swayed back and forth in time with each bark, paused between barks, and peeked at us to see if we were paying attention. We were pretty sure she enjoyed hearing herself bark, but when we laughed at her, she would become indignant.

My wife loves to putter around in the yard. If she plants it, it grows. The yard at the old house when we first got BooBoo was less than a half-acre and was planted to within an inch of its life. It wasn't overgrown, just filled up, and had something blooming all year around. Bromeliads are one of my wife's favorites, and she has moved her heirloom plants from one yard to the next practically her entire adult life. When we moved to the two acres in the country, we hauled two truckloads of plants and one truckload of furniture. She planted bromeliads under half the trees, a majority of which were in the front yard. Each tree had a different species, and most of them hold water in their centers. Not a great thing to have in Central Florida, because each little "cup" acts like a Petri dish of growth medium for mosquitos to flourish.

Mosquitos spawned more trouble for BooBoo, too. Ironically, the water in those Petri dishes relieved BooBoo's stomach ailments. Methodically circling every tree that had bromeliads, BooBoo stuck her nose into their centers and lapped up the liquid. Bromeliads have stiff, serrated leaves. Working them without gloves is a lot like having hand to paw combat with a cat; you will bleed. BooBoo's nose—raw, lacerated, and scarred—bore testament to her determination to self-medicate.

One day, while BooBoo nosed through the bromeliads, a particularly unfriendly neighbor walked one of her two dogs down our street. My wife and I had met her at a block party and came away with the same bad impression. BooBoo looked up from her therapy grazing, spotted the black herding-mix dog, and bolted straight for it before I could get between her and the street. The black dog cowered behind the woman. BooBoo shot between the lady's legs to get at the dog. It was momentary melee until I was able to wrangle BooBoo back into our yard. Fortunately, no physical damage occurred, but the prickly woman had been traumatized, sure that BooBoo had attacked her, not her dog.

Anyone who knew Booboo would have agreed that accusing her of attacking a person was preposterous. I thought that if she was to be charged with a crime, it needed to be the correct one. She loved people. It was dogs she couldn't stand.

My wife went over to the woman's house to apologize and explain BooBoo wasn't interested in her. While the woman wasn't going to call animal control, she did threaten us with a lawsuit if we didn't do something to "protect the neighborhood" from our "vicious" dog. Ailing as she was, BooBoo still looked imposing. AmStaff dogs are guilty until proven innocent.

I erected a real fence, separating the front plot from the rest of the yard, which cut BooBoo off from her favorite foraging grounds. She expressed her displeasure. Enablers that we were, we gave her an acceptable compromise: midnight raids. Supervised, she grazed after nine at night when surely no one would walk by. Pure luck.

As her condition slowly worsened, we discussed with the vet different medications for treating Cushing's. Collectively, we kept coming back to the same conclusion: the cure was as bad as, or worse, than the disease. We gave her over-the-counter meds for her digestive issues and, eventually, something for aches and pains, all of which were reducing her life expectancy, right along with the Cushing's.

We felt that our least bad choice was to keep her as comfortable as possible while she was here: keep her comfortable, keep her happy, enjoy her companionship as long as possible, and pay the price at the end. That was the plan.

Little did we know that the end would come sooner than we had anticipated.

We had been watching TV in the back room on the Thursday night before Sunday's Valentine's Day. BooBoo usually sat on the couch with us. Because she had lost so much muscle, she was having a hard time getting up. She finally made it but never got comfortable and got back down. Her search for a spot to lie down didn't seem to be going well. Then she started to dry heave. She soon threw up a large quantity of unprocessed dog food. We were alarmed not just because she had thrown up, but because she threw up so much and it was all undigested. Her second hurl brought up an even larger amount of raw food.

We were very concerned, but had no real plan of action. We kept an eye on her for a while. A little later she started to shiver all over. Time to call in the pros. Her vet was a neighbor and a friend who lived a little further back in the woods beyond our house. I called and he showed up in short order, and he didn't like what he saw. I followed him to his office with a confused BooBoo. He pumped fluids into her and sent her home about 11 p.m. with instructions to bring her back the next morning.

About an hour or so after we got home, BooBoo threw up again, only this time it was brown bile, not much of it but very thick and putrid. It was a very rough night. BooBoo could not get comfortable. She went from her bed to our bed to the floor and wandered all over the room. I let her out to pee, but all she wanted to do was to eat grass. I didn't want her to throw up again, so I shooed her back inside.

We skipped breakfast and were at the vet's at eight. He asked to keep her all day so he could do bloodwork and keep up her fluids. She never liked being at the vet's but didn't complain when I left her there. I returned to pick her up about six that night. She was still not feeling very spunky but was glad to get to go home. That night started out as bad as the one before: she had no luck finding a comfortable spot.

Around midnight, she settled into her bed. At 4 a.m., when I got up to see if she needed to go out to pee, she greeted me with a waggy tail and no more shivering. The vet had asked us to bring her back on Saturday morning to talk about any test results that may have come back and to top her off with fluids. He asked that I leave her there again. Not all of the results were back, but what he did have wasn't particularly good.

Around 10:30 a.m., we got a call to come and get her. The vet said she had told him she was ready to go home. She was weak, and car rides were never her thing, so the short trip home was not all that encouraging. The vet had instructed us to feed her small amounts of rice and a little water, spread out over the next day or so. Once home, she seemed to rally a little and barked at "mommy" for something to eat. She went outside and barked at a squirrel—one of her favorite things to do. Later that afternoon, she took advantage of my exhaustion and licked my face while I was napping, another of her favorite activities.

In the wee hours of Sunday morning, BooBoo crashed again, throwing up everything that she had consumed the afternoon before. It was obvious that food wasn't getting processed any more.

It was her time to go. We waited until 7 a.m. to call the vet at home. He picked up his bag at his office and was at our house in about an hour. He administered the sedative while she was lying on the living-room couch. Once it had taken effect, we moved her to a work bench in the garage, where he injected her with pentobarbital. She left us quickly and painlessly. The vet slipped out quietly to leave us with our goodbyes.

Without a doubt, letting her go was one of the most difficult things I have ever had to do. But we had to do it. It was her time to go.

In my mandated planning for this day, I had chosen a spot in our yard for her final resting place in front of a palm tree. She took great delight in chasing squirrels up that tree, jumping as high as she could, trying to climb the tree after them, barking the whole time.

My wife and I dug like we were possessed—no breaks, no slowing down—until her spot was ready. In the garage, we gently positioned her into the mattress slipcover from her crate, placed her on her comforter, folded it neatly around her, and carried her out to her chosen plot. Gathering ourselves, we lowered her to the bottom. Between sobs, we tossed handfuls of dirt on top of her comforter and struggled to say a few words. I finally settled on reciting the words to "Feeling Good," Nina Simone's anthem of liberation because BooBoo was now free from her pain and suffering. Shovels back in hand, we carefully filled in the hole around and over her and replaced the sod.

The rest of the day, we sobbed in our emptiness. We knew the usual trope: "She was better off. She no longer felt pain or suffering." We, on the other hand, had a long way to go before our grieving would subside enough to truly let her go and enjoy the memories of a truly sweet, innocent baby, our baby girl, who had graced us with her presence, and whom we had lost.

Dear Dr. Abbott

Dear Dr. Abbott,

    Thank you for taking such good care of me while I was in Glenwood. You are the nicest vet a three-year-old girl could ask for. Mommy always called me her precocious little three-year-old. Is "precocious" too big a word for me to know? Anyway, it was very nice of you to come to my house and trim my nails and stuff. I always got real nervous going to your office. And when I got sick at home this last week, you gave me a little more time with mommy and daddy. I got to bark at mommy and a squirrel and lick daddy's face. I think that it was kind of important to them and I liked it too.

    Thanks again for everything.

BooBoo

SALTY

Blues

They arrive with no warning or sign
They descend without reason or rhyme
And when they hit
I let myself sit
And wallow in gloom for a time

Oxpecker

Scavenging atop the scabious hide
for a meal of
parasitic hangers-on
is my abysmal existence.
Work sucks.
The food isn't great.
The ride goes nowhere.
Yet it is my lot in life.

What else am I to do?

Busted

I got caught.

In a somewhat rare lapse of decorum/judgment/personal protocol, yes rare, I did a one-eighty to appreciate a woman's gorgeous rear end as she walked down the concourse in the opposite direction.

At just that moment, she turned and caught me staring at her. She was not some young thing. She was mature, somewhere in that nebulous forties to fifties middle ground. We were still within hearing distance of each other. When she called me a pig, I stopped flatfooted. To my surprise, she stopped, too.

"Yes. Yes, I am," I retorted before she could take another swipe. "I'm a male chauvinist pig. I look at attractive women and appreciate their hard work and dedication to caring for themselves. I also open doors for them, pull out chairs for them, extend an arm for them. I tip my hat to them, and I stand up when they enter a room, join, or leave a table. I'm also capable of having a woman for a boss, voting for a woman president, and recognizing her as an equal. I believe that all of these actions make me the pig you refer to me as, and I believe that performing most of them is a lost art. Any man can stare, drool, wolf whistle, or behave rudely. Only a Chauvinist Pig can do it with disarming panache."

She softened her glare, gave me a slightly mischievous smile, a quick wink, whipped her head around, and continued down the concourse as if it were a catwalk.

I thought about giving her a wolf whistle, but decided that I had already pushed my luck far enough for one day.

Kintsugi

I'm tired
of gathering up the shards
that are my shattered self
strewn across the floor
after every crash
of sifting through each piece,
laboriously matching margins,
of using what little self-love
I have left
as the golden glue
to assemble a life
that is or isn't real.

I'm tired
of each time
it being that much more
burdensome to sift
smaller and smaller pieces,
of creating an order
recognizable not only
to others
but to myself,
of continuing the
charade of wellness
no matter how fine
the joinery.

I'm tired
of watching
others with means
trade old for new,
the rest of us making do
with the precious mettle
we have left.

I'm tired
of being amidst
each crash,
the next more horrific than the last,
more improbable to rejoin,
of having less and less
self-love
with which to
repair the vessel.

I'm tired
of the adjudication,
deciding what is whole,
what piece to meld back in,
what piece to leave out.
Who should make that call?
How do I determine
if I'm worth
the gold?

Current

It's time to run away again.
I can feel it.
That pull is unmistakably powerful,
like a rip current pulling me away from land.
When I was little,
my dad taught me how to get out
of that danger.
We summered on the Outer Banks,
where the rip currents were treacherous.
"Swim at your own risk. No lifeguards."
Once, I watched Dad save a young couple
struggling against that peril.
No big deal.
Swim parallel to land
until you're out of it,
then just swim back in.
I've been fighting this current,
swimming parallel, for a long time,
but the pull feels no less strong,
and Dad's no longer here to save me.
Every day that urge
to stop swimming
becomes more irresistible.
Let the current take me back out to sea!

Pets

I cry at the drop of a hat,
especially when it comes to my pets.
I mourned the loss of my parents
when they passed,
but I sobbed for weeks
when one of my pets died.
I guess I put a great deal of myself
into nurturing and loving them,
and they seem to appreciate it
much more than people do.

Life Is Short

Life is short.
It's used as a tag line in ads.
"Life's short; play hard."
It's used as a reminder.
"Life's short; take care of . . . whatever . . . now."

But then, every once in a while,
we're reminded of just what "life is short" really means.
We lose someone we love.
They depart unexpectedly,
even if they're in their nineties.

Our all-too-soft bodies—
Home Sweet Home during each incarnation—
seem fragile,
easily damaged
or broken,
or simply wear out,
sometimes way before they should,
or at least before we think they should.

Those of us who are left behind
feel caught off guard,
feel consumed by our grief.
We become angry
at losing someone dear to us,
at ourselves for having not said
or done
or been
something to someone

that they would have wanted
or needed
when we should have known.

Emerald Green

That vivid emerald green
of the new leaves
on the southern live oaks
is gone,
replaced by summer's
waxy dull green.
I barely saw the emerald,
much less enjoyed it,
a day at the most.
Feels a lot like my life.
I barely got to enjoy
any of it, really.
Of twenty-two thousand or more,
I seem to remember
about two dozen days
where I sat
in the twilight
and reflected,
"What a great day.
I really enjoyed myself."
Two dozen.
Maybe.
Where was I?
What was I doing?
Living?
Can it really
be called "living"
without the enjoying?
Shame on me
for not doing more

enjoying
and less
living.

Fleeting

Fleeting.
Brief.
White hot.
Known, yet unknown.
Explored, yet untouched.
Our love erupted with
such passion
it consumed me,
bathed me,
cleansed me
of my past.

Your love for me
was so pure,
so complete,
so unconditional,
I did not do it justice.
Yet I tried my best
to show you,
to give to you in return
my unconditional love.

I fear I fell short.

Wars have started
over far less.

Letting you go,
though one of the most
disconsolate things that
I have ever done,
was the thing that
I had to do.

Perhaps you will
return, free from
will and want.
One day.

Perhaps you and I
will never see
each other again.

But because of you,
I now know what
love is supposed to
feel like,
be like,
act like,
give like,
and take like.

I hope that
for your pain
you can find
some kernel of
something
that makes the
journey
worth the ache.

Like a recovering
alcoholic,
I will struggle to
put one more day
between us.

Not because I want to,
but because I have to.

And even though
I may not hold out
for you,
I will always hold on
to you.

The you that we were.

For even time
cannot take away
that from me.

The Alien

I once knew who I was.
I looked in the mirror
and recognized the person looking back.
That reflection matched the person I was.
I could look into those eyes and tell
who was who and what was what.
Sometimes the person
in the mirror needed a pep talk
or a reality check.
But he was always me,
on my side,
in my corner,
in it together.
But now I look in the mirror
and I see someone foreign.
I look into those eyes
and can't find the soul that I was,
much less the person that I am.
Instead, I see an imposter.
Someone pretending to be me
but who isn't.
Their eyes have dulled
Their skin has loosened,
wrinkled, and become blotched.
I'm still me.
Or at least I think I am.
But I have moved
into someone else's body.
So that makes me
the Alien.

Plagiarism. *The International Scholars Journal* defines it as the "wrongful appropriation," "close imitation" of another author's language, thoughts, ideas, or expressions, and the representation of them as one's own original work.

Plagiarism

If I'm feigning the motions of a job but not actually doing that job, and faking those motions well enough so as to make others believe I'm competent, even though I'm not actually doing that job at all, shouldn't that be considered a form of plagiarism?

If I behave the same way with relationships, isn't it plausible that should be viewed as plagiarism, too? And if my entire life has been this act of only going through the motions of living, mimicking others' words and deeds and not really participating in life itself, doesn't that constitute plagiarism of the highest order?

If you concur that appropriating someone else's life and calling it your own—an identity theft of sorts—is plagiarism, then I concede: I have co-opted from many that which I represent as my life. I have no originality whatsoever. I merely ape others. Worse yet, society views this behavior as an acceptable, nay, desirable, conformity—an initiation into the fold.

Those true occupiers of an original life, those who have dared to put forward original ideas, who have made original choices, and who have spoken their beliefs with individuality have been labeled as societal outcasts, or worse.

Defying convention, Galileo Galilei insisted: "And yet it does move."

P.S. I'm an international inquirer. I thought so might you be. With gratitude to *Scientific American*, I have discovered that those infamous words may not after all have escaped the lips of the great Italian mathematician, philosopher, and astrophysicist Galileo Galilei (1564–1642) when forced in 1633 by the Catholic Church to recant his heretic heliocentric theory—that the Earth revolves around the sun and not—as the Church taught—that the Earth is the center of the universe. Tortured and under threat of being burned at the stake, Galileo was persuaded to abjure his life's work before a court of Inquisitors. At the end of the six-year-long ordeal, he might have muttered those words under his breath—as he most-assuredly thought them—but they would have been inaudible to his judge and jury.

In actuality, the phrase appeared more than a century after Galileo's death in the 1757 book *The Italian Library*, published in London by Italian author Giuseppe Baretti. Supposedly, the moment the Inquisition set Galileo free, the physicist looked up to the sky, down to the ground and, stomping his foot on the earth, he vilified his theory: *Eppur si move* (still, it moves). The Earth under his feet did, indeed, revolve around the sun.

But the complex story that emerged remains timely and relevant, for we say what we dare and do what we must to make our way through this world, with hope, intact. Mostly. To these conclusions I abjure: there *is* nothing new under the sun. Therefore, we are all plagiarists.

Christmas Cheer

I'm in the mood to tell a story, but there's no one here to tell it to, so I'm going to tell it to you, not that you're no one.

It's about my friend Harrison and his Christmas party. Harrison and I had been crewing that fall on a small, one-design sailboat that was campaigning throughout the southeast, and we became friends.

Harrison was a psychology professor at the local state college that I was attending, or was going to attend—I've lost the exact time frame—but it was after number one and before number two (wives, that is), and after my first stint and before my second pass at getting a college education. He was living in the house where we would build his thirty-foot-long, double-ended commercial fishing boat, so that puts it somewhere around '78 or '79.

Harrison's reputation with women preceded him. I had seen first-hand how women fluttered about him like hummingbirds around a sugar-water feeder. I even had the good fortune of having one or two of them land on my arm for a moment or two, I'm sure only because they had tired of flitting around him. I had not yet been privy to the full extent of his charms. All of that was about to change.

It was Christmas Eve. Harrison invited me to a small party at his house. "Nothing formal, no need to bring a thing. Do come early so you don't miss anything," he said. I showed up before dark. His son, Brandon, his daughter (whose name eludes me), his brother, Benny, Benny's wife (ditto on the name thing), and Harrison's ex, Pandora, all greeted me. It seemed odd that Harrison's ex would be there, but she turned out to be a prominent character throughout the rest of his life, even though they never remarried.

Now that I think more about the timing, it had to have been before my wife number one and after my mis-spent semester at Syracuse—around '75. While wasting a semester at Syracuse, a guy living on my dorm floor turned out to be an acquaintance from my past. For my first thirteen years, I lived in a suburb of Pittsburgh. When I was old enough, our next-door neighbor would take me upstate to a sailing club where he was a member. The guy on my dorm floor turned out to be a guy I used to hang out with at that club. Small world.

After my family moved to Florida, I had forgotten about sailing and that type of boat. Reconnecting with this guy rekindled my interest. I looked up the Florida fleet and hooked up with a skipper out of Jacksonville.

That's when I met Harrison. Massive calves. Tree-trunk thighs. Beer-barrel torso and arms to match. Handsome, devilish grin. Wicked sense of humor. A world-class cynic. We hit it off right away.

At his Christmas party, I met other guests: one of Harrison's fellow professors, one of his son's friends.

Then the show began. A tall blond in the cocktail dress with beautifully styled hair, red nails, and a little too much jewelry and perfume, arrived carrying an overnight bag. Harrison had designated Brandon as the doorman and had obviously coached him on how to execute his duties. As the woman entered the room, Brandon blocked her view of its occupants. Like a stage curtain slowly opening, Brandon inched to one side, revealing the guests . . . one at a time.

Harrison had strategically placed himself in the back of the room so that he would be the next to last person the blond would see as she panned the space. The last person would be Harrison's ex. The effect was trenchant; nay, brutal. Her face changed from pensive as she looked for Harrison to excited when she finally found him to confused and crestfallen when she saw his ex.

The event appeared to be perfectly choreographed. She dropped her bag by the door, made her way across the room, and attempted to pull Harrison "off stage" to have a word with him in private. He would have none of it. He remained rooted to his spot as if he had grown there.

The awkward silence receded and conversations resumed.

Ten minutes later, the doorbell announced Act Two.

A tall brunette, a little thinner, a little more casual, also carrying an overnight bag, same slow reveal, same poised reaction, except that she had one additional face to face. The same silence fell on the room as we watched the train wreck. Jockeying for space, proximity, and attention became intense.

It seemed to me that any other man would be on his bicycle, attempting to avoid all the land mines that he had set, but not Harrison. He remained detached and cool. Aloof, but not rude. Pandora stayed in her place: stage far right.

Another ten minutes, raise the curtain on Act Three. This time, the room went quiet before Brandon reached the door. Girlfriend number three arrived—shorter than the other two, less makeup, less jewelry, no noticeable perfume, the obligatory overnight bag in hand. She made short work of reading the room and headed straight for the kitchen and a drink.

I would play Sir Galahad later that night to this girl's inebriated Maid Marian. I suspected Harrison had choreographed that, too, although he hadn't clued me in on that strategy in advance.

The party continued. More drinks, more circling, more tension. Each of the three women arrived that night fully anticipating spending the night with Harrison. Instead, they were pitted against each other and vied for the same prize. In some ways, it was painful to watch; in others, it was impossible not to. The standoff went on for several hours.

About 10 p.m., the air in the room changed. It took me a second or two to figure out what had happened. Pandora had excused herself rather quietly and retreated to Harrison's bedroom, locking the door. Game over. To this day I have no idea what role Pandora was assigned, if any. She could have been one of the "contestants," but I doubted it. Her role was more likely that of closer. Being Harrison's ex, and knowing him better than the rest, she allowed him his fun, then dropped the hammer.

The blonde and the brunette said their goodbyes and left. The third woman tried to extract some sort of response from Harrison by being extra attentive to me, which I had no shame in fully exploiting.

At that Christmas party, Harrison had cleaned house of all his girlfriends for that year to take up with a new batch. A few years later, he settled on one in particular. They designed a house together and planned a future. I felt a little sorry for that one, and for me as well. Harrison deftly freed himself of her by having me steal her away. I had been set up, of course. My inexperience and ego led me to believe that I had, indeed, stolen her from a master playboy.

She turned out to be my ex- number two. I'll save that story for another day.

Crushed

Good grief.
What do you think this is,
some sort of hopey-feely
meritocracy?
This is America, man,
where the rich get richer,
the poor get poorer,
and the little guys
have their dreams
crushed out of them
like
orange juice pulp.

Deflection

I joined a childhood friend for a libation the other day.
His hospitality and home were both so warm and soothing.
We chattered on about life's many twists and turns.
Sometime during the conversation,
I let my hoary shield down.

He took it upon himself to ask, "What burdens you, old friend?"
for he had perceived the pitch of my shoulders.
I hadn't the courage to tell him "Nothing,"
as in "You're just looking at the true me,
a sad, shrunken nut confined in an oversized shell."
Instead, I smiled and said, "Nothing,"
as in "I'm fine," and quickly reaffixed my shield.

Later, we joined others at the dinner table,
all shields adroitly in place,
bravado sloshing about like the drinks.

Afterwards, all alone,
I thought longingly about the emancipation
my dear friend had availed me:
to cede my armor,
And hang that heavy shield upon his wall.

Her

The hour approaches midnight.
We sit in our own sweat.
We cannot speak.
We cannot sleep.
We try to lie down.
but we can only weep.

Years ago, we would have fought,
trading abusive obscenities.
Now we cannot speak.
We sit and stare.
We try to lie down,
but we no longer care.

The hour approaches one,
and, in that time, I've nodded off,
while death has taken her,
I cannot sleep.
I try to lie down,
but I can only weep.

Hypocrisy II

They do love a brother what make an athletic feat
but hate that Black family who moved in down the street.
It's just fine what *he* do with that pigskin.
They just don't like the color of *their* dark skin.
Love that tall Muslim makin' their nets go swish,
but hate the Islamic culture makin' their own niche.
Their god created all of Eden's creatures,
just better not have some sorta odd features.
If it don't match what they see in the mirror,
they run the opposite way, galvanized by fear.
Their good book be tattered and well-read,
but in the end, they rather not see the wealth be spread.

The Circle

Cold, gray, and waxen,
immersed in the dying pool,
he lies suspended,

drawn up to the living
Only long enough to respond,
then slowly returned.

Held there in this twilight
He repairs.

For him, time is removed.
For us, seconds are forever.
Cruelly contorting hours into days,
Days into weeks.

We wait,
watching everything,
wondering

How . . .

how has our once mighty protectorate
come to this?

The answer is history.
The future offers no hope

We,
as mere mortals,
cannot cheat

Time.

Amusement Park

I am a soul, inhabiting a life form, just like all of the other souls on this planet. At present, I happen to reside in the body of what is referred to as *Homo sapiens*, or human. Other souls reside in other forms with common names like oxpecker or tiger or dolphin or squirrel or ant or . . . you get the picture . . . all of us . . . souls.

We inhabit a rock that circles a heat source. On this rock, souls are affected by the form they inhabit. For example, my human form. What a murderous lot many humas are. The human form seems intemperate and takes great pleasure in annihilating each other. *Homo sapiens* are not only homicidal, but they also destroy other life forms on this rock with zealousness and reckless abandonment. Humans seem not to have any compunction about *what* is killed. Some just seem to be driven by an overriding need *to* kill with whatever weapon of destruction is available. Stomp, wring, choke, stab, club, shoot, run over with machinery, exterminating whatever appears to have no value to them.

The instinct to kill is strong. I myself have capitulated to that urge on a few regretful occasions—although never unleashing my impulse on another human being, at least not yet. I've thought about terminating the existence of those I consider malevolent humans. Do you suppose there's greater satisfaction in interspecies extermination?

I mostly want to expunge those that take pleasure in harming others and things. I think they've lost their way. Maybe a re-programing would be more appropriate. Perhaps they need to be freed of their current human bindings and go back to seeing themselves as souls waiting to inhabit an entity—entities that are unique but the same.

It could be that such thoughts are naïve and give away that I may be new to this human form. Maybe these other souls have been embedded into the human form too long, too many times. Maybe they've become desensitized and lost the ability to feel any deep connection to other souls—in all forms.

I'm not exactly sure why we souls are here, inhabiting such an array of life forms on this particular rock in this particular part of the universe or even in this universe at all. Surely, the reason for our presence isn't to shorten the experience of any other presence. Or maybe it is.

Maybe that's only the way things look from the shooting gallery in the amusement park called Earth that is but one ride in a giant universe park. Just another daytrip.

Maybe this *Homo sapiens* experience is too wild a ride, and I need to find one tamer. I wonder what they do in the next galaxy over?

Virtue

This time, I have lost myself in her light-blue eyes. I want to fall in and swim there for hours. Mysteriously, she is rapt by my stare, seemingly captivated. Her reciprocal interest catches me off guard. That I may be even partially responsible for this striking redhead's pleasure as we engage, her gaze is heady stuff.

I have wasted no seconds imagining the sensation of her soft, full lips (that are now forming a totally infectious smile). The rest of her is equally inspiring. Sensual. Sexual. Slinky. Paradoxically, her innocent manner puts me totally at ease with my arousal. I'm alert to the allure and want. She is dangerously disarming. I want to spit risk in the face.

Since that first encounter, she has consumed my dreams. Waking, desire and propriety do battle. Some days, I think that we have turned the corner: rampant lust has mellowed into intellectual intercourse. I kid myself. I walk a minefield of temptations. From where comes my sudden rectitude and capacity not to wander into rapturous moments of moist flesh on flesh? Have I lost my mind, which is often lodged elsewhere?

I am not a Tin Man. Did the Wizard give me a heart? Or did Dorothy steal my balls when I wasn't looking?

BITTER

Death by Ducks

O, tortured soul, rest.
O, that I may tonight,
be it slumber or death,
let me retire from the fight.

Days run together such that
I cannot tell one from next.
Tasks demanded seem never to cease,
and the ducks . . . they nibble and vex.

Not one strike with labrys
brought Minoans asunder,
but compounded ten by ten,
axes fell the stoutest lumber.

I am tired . . . oozing much.
Yet each morn I rise to battle,
for faith of one makes faith of all,
though waging war is senseless rattle.

Each night I seek sanctuary,
hoping for sleep's cure,
binding the slivers of my splintered soul,
as I've made promise to endure.

Splits

Blank pages
Blank thoughts
Silent rages
Bad things wrought

Things look bleak
Times are low
Someone must speak
Something must blow

What did I do?
What happened today?
Why have you withdrawn?
Why have you run away?

When

Each day,
in the late afternoon,
when the sun turns from
bright white
to gold
to pale yellow
and then,
finally, to burnt orange
before gracefully lowering
himself into the west,
I die just a little.

I can't help but feel
the chill of death
when this life-giving star
pulls darkness over light
like a sheet over a corpse.
The blackness heightens the sense
of my mortality

I'm well past noon.

Blanket Notice

Dear Sir or Madam,
We regret to inform you that
your (choose one: Father, Son, Spouse,
Ex, Friend, Enemy, Other)
has met with an untimely end
at his own hands.

Best we can tell,
he left because
he was too old
to find suitable work
and too young to
retire to the life he wished
to become accustomed to.
In other words,
he died from laziness.

He is survived by
two biological parents
who are quite sure that they
were supposed to go first
but didn't;
one spayed/neutered cat
who finds it damn inconvenient
that he didn't give
two-weeks' notice;
one dog
who will miss the deceased
but who is already sleeping
on the deceased's side of the bed;
two birds

who no longer have a whistling
partner in the other room
(birds prefer anonymity, anyway);
one spouse
who is grateful that
the deceased moved
funds prior to departure
and left no stain;
one son
who didn't get the inheritance necessary
to live a life of ease;
one ex
whose son was shorted,
she's sure;
one friend
who will fill the void with a forty-pound
sack of potatoes;
one enemy
who will now
need to get over it
(you know who you are);
and one "other."

RIP

Mr. Eric

He came to us as Eric the Red,
tail straight up in the air,
slight question mark at the very tip.
Proud.
Fierce.
Hunter.
Warrior.
Twelve-plus pounds
of badass puddy,
commander of all he saw,
demanding,
"Do it my way or get the claw."
We were just staff.
Curmudgeon,
Grumpapotamus
slowly warmed.
We became pals.
He sought my lap,
wanted my pats
(I learned to do it right).
I poured my heart into him.
He loved me back
. . . in his own way.
It was all that I could expect.
It was more than I ever hoped for.
I miss him like crazy.

More Friend than I Deserve

You all know how this one goes:
you have a friend you don't deserve,
you didn't earn,
yet there he is
with cheer to burn.

You call him up; he'll talk blue streaks
about the wind, the rain, or snow.
Your carp and howl
of all things dark
he simply won't allow.

When black clouds hover overhead,
his sunshine burns them off.
You spin your despair
as a sticky web?
Those never have a prayer.

And what do you offer in return
for such a friend's compassion?
A cheery disposition?
That's a stretch
even for a magician.

Pound Sand

The omnipresent oppression of life
slowly grinds you
back into the
earth from
whence
came
you

D
U
S
T

Oldies

All my music has become too painful.
Each of the songs carry memories of their own.
They expose old bones that I thought had knitted.
Their lyrics make me rue my life
and wish for a different outcome.
I miss my house,
my warm floors and big windows,
looking out on a blank canvas.
All those wrong turns
underscored by lyrics
seemingly written just for me.
I should imbue myself with new releases
and leave those oldies to molder.

Counterintelligence

It's not easy being an observer and a bystander who feels helpless to change much of humankind's outrageously egotistical, vitriolic, and even murderous tendencies evidenced in every society—across the planet. We don't seem to know what we're capable of if and when we snap.

We probably don't see ourselves as infectious agents—a virus that multiplies once it's hijacked its host cell. Consider this: viruses eventually kill the very cells they need to survive. It's counterintuitive and counter intelligent. It's a kill-or-be-killed battle. But we err if we think that the only way to survive and thrive means taking over our host.

More and more, we behave like impetuous children. Rather than practicing tolerance, patience, and good stewardship, we act out selfishly. The singular "me" has become far more important than the collective "we." The American Psychological Association defines "acting out" as "the behavioral expression of emotions that serves to relieve tension associated with these emotions or to communicate them in a disguised, or indirect, way to others. Such behaviors may include arguing, fighting, stealing, threatening, or throwing tantrums. In psychoanalytic theory, reenactment of past events as an expression of unconscious emotional conflicts, feelings, or desires—often sexual or aggressive—with no conscious awareness of the origin or meaning of these behaviors."

That's comprehensive enough to capture the gamut of our inhumanity, not only to fellow humans but also to all life on this planet. My conjecture is that many of us are driven by the misguided belief that we're the keepers of superiority with a self-appointed mandate to control and wield power over all things once ascribed to a Creator. All around is incontrovertible evidence to the contrary. We have no such right, no such mandate, except to protect human rights and the rights of all things animate and inanimate, including the planet itself.

What keeps us from fulfilling our stewardship destiny? Fear. Fear of change. Fear of loss. Fear of being less than anyone else. And greed. These beliefs trigger all-encroaching maleficence.

Somehow, someone twisted Genesis, which puts forth the human mandate to not only to be fruitful and multiply and have dominion over living creatures, but to recognize that with dominion comes the huge responsibility to function as caretaker of the earth and all its creatures for all generations.

Instead of guarding, we're killing. Humans, animals, soil, water, air. For pride, greed, sexual gratification, for the sheer psychotic pleasure and perversion of domination in all its negative aspects devoid of the responsibility of stewardship.

It isn't just individuals. Corporations can and do become maleficent as well, placing profits and growth ahead of stewardship, plundering of the planet's resources along the way, arguing, "We know what's best for our shareholders."

What virtues make us worthy of the gift we've been given? Love. Integrity. Empathy. Respect. Honesty. Courage. Humility. Gratitude. Justness. Fairness. Generosity. Inspiring. Equanimity. Trustworthiness. Truthfulness. Patience. Wisdom.

If there is no pushback—no antibodies—against the invaders, no raising of the collective conscience to know when to say "enough is enough," then, maybe, it's best that our planet shed itself of its virus before this plague contaminates any other part of the universe.

Passing Notes

Now may be just as good
an inappropriate time
as any
to tell all of you
to leave me the fuck alone
if you find that I'm dying . . .
of anything.

Hoist a beer to my life
or death
as you see fit after I'm gone.
But don't try to wallow
in the experience with me
while I'm in the midst
of passing from here to there.

Laugh, cry, love,
and live with good friends,
but die like cats or elephants.
Go it alone
and pass with dignity and,
one would hope,
a great deal of serious drugs.

I raise my stein
and offer
the first toast
to our fallen friends.
Here's to them all!

Gray Man

I am not sick,
    but I am not well.
I am not good,
    but I am not bad.
I am not old,
    but I am not young.
I have become
    a shade
        of gray,
showing up each morning
    only because
        I should,
more watcher than participant,
    with less interest
        in the outcome
            each passing day.

The list of things needs doing
                grows.
The desire to accomplish them
wanes.
I no longer care.
    But no one else cares that I don't.

Each morning the distance to go seems longer,
    while the time allotted seems shorter.

Sucking up resources with wearisome repetitiveness,
    yet producing less and less in payment for their costs,
      in-between,
        marking time,
          I have become
            a shade
              of gray.

Oil

If we were to
drill down
to our core,
we would discover
that we are
what we are,
what we were,
and what we always
will be.

No amount of spot remover
will ever change the leopard.

No two weeks,
nor twenty-eight days,
nor twelve steps
will ever undo
what was,
from nascency, set.

We learn
to live within,
not actually
re-wire.

Slothfulness,
procrastination,
unchecked anger.

When drilled to our core,
put under duress,
all that can
be extracted
is what is there
to begin with.
Our essence.

Two-Tone

Bathed in black and white,
he picks no bones,
he sees no muted tones,
strictly wrong or right.

Columns stacked straight and true,
life's little choices
have no voices,
no accommodation for the blues.

Bathed in black and white,
a politician he is not.
He does not travel deep in thought.
He finds himself at home most every night.

A simple mind, or so some say,
a gentle soul
who pays no toll,
for at the end of every day,

he's bathed in black and white.

The Wicked Witch

The Wicked Witch of Twoville
called today
just to say,
"My life is far better than your own."
At least that was the gist of it,
but much more drawn out.
Details, darling,
are what twist the knife:
how she traveled,
where she went,
and whom she saw.
It all matters,
at least to her.
And I let it get to me . . .
every single time.

Escape Clause

This all started when—while sitting at my tiny little desk, crammed into a tiny little cubical, lost in the middle of an unending sea of thousands of little cubicles, located in the bowels of the place—an announcement came over the public address system.

"Paging Mr. Conway. Paging Mr. Edwin S. Conway. Please report to the Big Boss, Level 1, Suite ♭, at once."

I stood, peered over the tops of the unending rows of cubicles and tried to re-orient myself. Bearings gaining, I headed down the hall toward the bank of elevators. Heads behind cubicles popped up like prairie dogs peering out of their burrows. Eyes burned holes in the back of my head as I passed by, then quickly ducked back into their cubes lest the powers that be label them as slackers.

A vague wave of nausea churned in my stomach. I racked my brain, trying to think of something that I might have screwed up in the past month, two months, year. Nothing came to mind that would warrant a chat with the Big Boss.

I pressed the elevator "UP" button, stepped into the first doors that opened, turned, and pressed "1." The doors closed silently, and up I went. Level 1 was a long way up. The speed of the fast elevator didn't do anything to relieve that queasy feeling in the pit of my stomach. I felt the motion stop. I had reached Level 1. The doors opened as silently as they had closed. I stepped into a bright, antiseptically sterile-looking hallway. The view to the left was identical to the one on the right, both uninterrupted to the vanishing point.

Pick one, I thought, in the absence of signs. I headed down the left hall. The presumed office doors were far enough apart that it took a while to realize that the glyphs on them, although not in any alphabet I recognized, appeared to be ascending. I reversed course and trudged down the hall in the other direction. I should have packed a lunch. The nomenclature on these doors were definitely descending, but it was a long walk exacerbated by my feeling of dread.

Finally, I saw the end of the hall with double doors in the middle. As I approached, I could see the single glyph identifying the suite. Inside was a mid-sized waiting area, well-appointed with comfortable-looking sofas and chairs, a few coffee tables, reading materials scattered on them, but devoid of anyone. At the far end, a receptionist sat behind a desk. As I approached to announce myself, the receptionist gave me an almost imperceivable nod, and the door to the right clicked and opened a crack.

Hand on the knob, I took a deep breath and stepped into a room that didn't appear to be as big as the waiting room from which I had just come. Two smallish, nondescript chairs sat in front of what I assumed was a desk, a medium-sized, clear thin piece of glass supported by architectural legs. No phone. No paper. No "in" box. Nothing on its surface. Just clear glass. The walls were blank. As I neared, the man behind the desk stood, leaned forward, and extended his hand.

"Mr. Edwin . . ." He paused, glanced down at the spotless glass surface as though checking notes, then met my eyes. "Mr. Edwin S. Conway?"

"Yes," I acknowledged, pointing to my initials, ESC, embroidered on the handkerchief dapperly peeking from my suit breast pocket, and then shaking his cool hand.

"Well, I'm glad you're finally here, Mr. Conway. I've been looking for you."

He walked around the desk, strode past me, and headed for the door. Reaching a hat rack, which I hadn't noticed when I came in, he continued. "As is our tradition, Mr. Conway, I will keep this brief. Ever since our founder started this place, he instilled in his successor the principle of efficacy—know enough about each ward to match them with a drudgery that will test their resilience and expand their boundaries of endurance during their tenure with us.

"In so doing," he continued, "our founder had the prescience to ensure a lineage of successors. And by following this principle, each successor was, in turn, able to find his own successor, and on down the line . . . right up to now, Mr. Conway. For now, I have found . . . you."

He lifted his hat off the rack, placed it firmly on his head, tipped its brim slightly in my direction, turned, and walked out the door that moments before I had walked through. Gone.

"Successor? Successor to what?" I asked the empty room. I rushed to open the door he had just exited, intending to ask him questions, but the reception room was now filled with murmuring people, none of whom were the man in the hat. On seeing me, the room went stone quiet. All eyes fixed on this strange new figure stupefied by events not of his understanding.

"Your next appointment is waiting, sir," the receptionist said to me. "Shall I send them in?"

I retreated and closed the door . . . my door it seemed, behind me. Panic crept in. I desperately tried to make sense of what had just happened when a voice interrupted my thoughts. A disembodied voice, which seemed to come from everywhere, announced that Sector Eight was on the line and wished to speak to me about something urgent. This development quickly spiraled out of control. My head was reeling.

"Tell them I'll call them back," I muttered.

"Yes, sir," responded the disembodied voice. The room was once again silent. I paced like a deranged inmate plotting his escape.

After a minute or two of wandering around the sterile box—who knows how long?—I sank into the chair on the far side of the desk, propped my elbows on its surface, and buried my head into my hands.

This makes no sense . . . no sense at all . . . and what's that beeping?

I opened my eyes to look for the source of the noise. For the first time, I noticed that the desk wasn't the clear, thin sheet of glass I thought it was. It looked like some sort of high-tech nuclear reactor control panel. Blinking lights, gauges, and graphs filled its surface, except for a small, blank space in the lower middle. The panic that had been nibbling at the edges of my consciousness had now engulfed me. I felt like I was being squeezed by a boa constrictor. How perfect was that? All my life I've been petrified of snakes.

Pushing away from the desk, I paced the room some more. A few deep breaths enabled me to start thinking rationally. I recounted what had happened.

I was called to the Big Boss's office, where he said something about the company founder's procedure for establishing a line of successors. Suddenly, I was alone in the boss's office, with no reasonable expectation of him returning. Therefore, I must be . . . the Big Boss.

That last realization ricocheted around in my brain, lighting up synapses, much like all of the lights blinking on that damn glass desk. Let me see if I can provide you with a proper characterization of myself. I'm an atheist—or so I thought—convinced of no heaven, conversely, no hell. Furthermore, I was sure that if I was wrong, I wouldn't be going to heaven, anyway, and not just because I didn't believe in it. Best as I could make of it, hell is where they match you up with your biggest dread, your worst nightmare, your least-liked task, and then make you perform that task over and over, forever.

But somehow, the Original Boss, maybe an attorney, maybe a proto-attorney, introduced an "Escape Clause," a loophole, that assure equal parts of hope and indentured servitude. *Find your successor, then you're out.* Out to "where" is yet to be determined, but there is an "out," nonetheless.

Surviving the initial shock of being designated as a successor, I dug in, mastered the control center disguised as a clear glass-top desk, and fell into the routine of being the Big Boss.

Don't get me wrong, being the boss has its perks. I redecorated, creating a luxurious office. Now, paintings by blue-chip artists hang on the walls. Sculptures sit on pedestals. A craftsman fabricated a lovely view of whatever I want to view, which I can change on a whim. There are some truly masterful artists who work here.

Best of all, I get to make all the decisions. The downside is I *have* to make all the decisions. And all of them are difficult. And they are non-stop. I can't not make them, and bad decisions make things worse. Another downside to being the boss is that I never, ever, ever, get to leave. There are no breaks. There is no going home. There is "no rest for the wicked," as they say. Maybe I have become the wicked.

But I am constantly on the lookout for my own little loophole. My ESC clause. My successor must be out there somewhere. After all, my predecessor found one, didn't he?

UMAMI

Small Talk

I long for your touch,
sensual at its tip,
unhurried, languid,
the intensity of the pleasure
only for pleasure's sake,
not brought to fruition,
for I am serving time,
which in and of itself
seems a secondary crime,
a waste of something near and dear,
a loss of a natural resource
on an unnatural edifice.

I while away this sentence,
thinking of what could be
between you and me.
Small talk,
silken fingertips,
filling every precious moment
full of nothing.

Have I mentioned that I miss you?

Neurosis

I don't know why
I can't just be morose
all by myself
and leave it at that.
But for some reason,
I think that I need to
share with others,
put into words,
my bleakness,
to spout great prose of angst,
which, unfortunately, this is not.
Pain compels me to try,
so I write.
Long and short,
patterned and blank,
light and dark.
Excise the pain,
at least a little.
But for all the effort,
my despair refuses to take wing
as I so desperately need for it to.
I don't want therapy.
I want a rhythmic benefaction
to spatter the canvas with
lexicons of language,
to evoke emotions,
to let readers hear the dog's breath
and feel its snarl,
to string together
carefully crafted originality,
individuality,

to express the ineffable,
and tempt even the littérateur
to give a little nod in my direction,
if only to say,
"He tries too damn hard."

My Son

Our hours are measured in weeks.
You grow in spurts,
the difference noticeable
from one week to the next.
Your highs and lows
I see out of context.

I'm relegated to rooting
for the home team while
it plays away games.
Yet, it would be unfair of me
to lay blame for these things
upon a single set of shoulders.

I stand outside looking in.
I anticipate the falls.
I see the crashes in replay.
Their noises reach me
long after the occurrence has past
and there are gaps in us.

Judgment of your deeds,
both good and not-so-great,
is left open to interpretation
too long after the fact.
I wish only that you succeed,
waiting for our reunions to tell you.

What choice have we except
to work through those things
that life brings to us,
although they may seem unfair?
For it is trial and tribulation,
my son,
that turns the cub into the bear.

Ideas

I got permutations runnin' out my head,

they havin' babies.   spillin' all 'round the floor.

got so many maybes   I come up with

My Ideas   any more

ifs,

they'll be

burstin' thru

the door,

runnin' down

the street,

askin' everyone

they meet,

"Can you compete?"

'cause this one

goin'

nowhere.

Ideas?

The Bear

I saw the bear,
and the bear saw me.
He did not seem to care,
though he did stop and stare
and kind of glare
at me
before lumbering back to the woods
to
do that thing that bears do in the woods,
just like me.

Attendant

Disembarking from the penultimate plane of a multi-leg trip where each airport had blurred into a similarity with the last, I was in need of a restroom. Those, too, have a homogeneity: same general location, same layout, same tile, same smell. Perhaps so that the dazed traveler doesn't have to think too hard.

Entering, I was met by an attendant who stood just inside. Finding someone "attending" an airport restroom was jarring enough, but this man had to have been in his early seventies, and he looked like he really needed the job.

Threadbare but clean suit. Thin black tie. Small billowing wisps of white hair, well back from his brow, looking for all the world like a personal lenticular cloud hovering above him. Spectacles—for that's really all you could call them, two small lumps of glass wrapped in wire—perched partway down the bridge of his nose.

He was weathered in an eroded-by-the-labors-of-life kind of way, yet still straight-backed. His English—heavy with a Middle-European accent—was sparse and halting. His fixed smile revealed teeth in need of some dental attention: stained, but not rotting, still serviceable, not unpleasant, and obviously his own.

Thrown off by his unexpected presence, I quickly skirted around him and searched for an opening, all the while listening to him—in his broken English—greet other arrivals and acknowledge those leaving. He had the demeanor of someone who was there not out of boredom but out of requirement, not unhappy with his plight but resigned to it. He worked his little sphere of influence professionally, acknowledging all who entered and left as if the room was attached to an exclusive nightclub and he vied for correlating tips.

As I exited the restroom, I looked him in the eyes, gave him a nod, and pressed a five into his hand. This could well be me with very little change in happenstance. If, one day, I did find myself in his shoes, I would want someone to give me that same courtesy and press a five into my hand, for I would surely need it.

Democrats

I was snug in my bed when the doorbell rang in the middle of the night. As I wondered if I was having a lucid dream, I shuffled to the front door in nothing more than my baby blue briefs. The lanky young man with a blond goatee standing under the porch light—a university-student type—didn't seem to notice.

"Wake up!" he said. "Smell that?"

"Did you fart?" I asked.

"That's not your morning coffee brewing—that's your house on fire. Look around. See all of those people with an "R" emblazoned on their red caps and T-shirts?"

It was too dark to see anyone, except the Donaldsons' Doberman squatting on my front lawn.

"Those are Republicans. They don't want you in their village. They don't want you to have a village. They don't want you to have a say in your life. They want to take away your rights. In fact, they've already started by marginalizing you, by gerrymandering your districts, by limiting your access, by dividing you."

I didn't feel divided. Maybe my baby blue briefs gave that impression.

"You must fight back! You must vote in every election and vote Democratic. Vote for the Democrat running for dog catcher. Vote for the Democrats running for town council, city council, mayor, school board, county commissioner, and AG. Vote for the Democrats running for State House and State Senate and Judge of the Court of Common Pleas. Vote for the Democrats running for governor and U.S. House of Representative and the U.S. Senate. Vote for the Democrat running for President of the United States—our United States."

He stretched out his hands as though he was offering me a pizza. "Don't like everything about them? Hold your nose and vote for them anyway. We have to push back. This doesn't get accomplished by someone else. This gets accomplished by you and you alone."

He pointed a finger at my bare chest, which, by now, was covered in goose bumps. I wondered what "this" was that was so urgent at 2:30 a.m.

"YOU MUST GET OUT AND VOTE!" he shouted.

I was afraid he was going to wake the McConnells. At least he scared the Doberman away.

"These are not nice people. These are not sane, rational people. These are people that HATE YOU. Your only defense against them is to vote them into abeyance. VOTE! VOTE! VOTE!"

I kept wondering when he was going to get to the point.

"You can no longer afford to sit on the sidelines. This is a classic case of 'use it or lose it.' Every last person eligible to vote must do so. Victory takes numbers. Success is achieved by showing up—en mass. Each and every Democrat and Independent must come to the polls, must display a show of solidarity, of unity that will hammer home the point—that we are fed up and won't take it anymore. Republicans don't want to work across the aisle. They don't want to give us our rightful place at the table, so we have to take it back by force. By numbers! By voting! VOTE! VOTE! VOTE!"

"I'm sorry, I didn't get that," I said.

"VOTE! VOTE! VOTE!"

He handed me a slick flyer, turned, and disappeared into the night. I liked his goatee.

V

Tuesday,
always Tuesday,
never Sunday
or Friday
or even Wednesday,
but always on Tuesday
they come by.
They never stay long,
just long enough to ensure that
they have been seen.
Then off they go,
flocking
to parts unknown
to gaggle somewhere else.
It seemed strange at first.
But we got used to them
V-ing in and meandering about,
like I said,
just long enough to
to be seen
then V-ing back out.
Maybe they're creating an alibi,
planning this grand heist
of corn in someone else's field.
Or maybe they're just social
but a little shy,
building up their nerve to actually
stay a while.
They'll always be welcome.

A Pet of My Own

I've got an empty pillow
where my honey oughta be
'cause she's still outside a-readin'
near our weeping willow tree.

The dog is always with her
no matter where she goes,
so I'm always flyin' solo,
overcoming my life's lows.

Even that ungrateful cat
I've become the door man for
only wants his mama
'cause he thinks I'm such a bore.

Need to find my own companion,
something loyal, cuddly, and soft.
I'm still attracted to the bunnies,
with December's fur coat doffed.

That Stuff

How do you feel?
Feel?
From the meal?
From the ordeal?
No. The meal . . .
of veal.
Oh. What an ordeal.
Ordeal?
The veal!
Prepping the meal?
The whole ordeal!
Ordeal?
The meal . . .
of veal!
Oh! That ordeal.
I'm stuffed!

Alexandria, Louisiana

In 1990, wife number two and I moved from Orlando, Florida, to Rome, Georgia. She had accepted a position as office manager for a group of heart surgeons who were going to build their own clinic. I left my job as construction manager with Walt Disney World, knowingly without a job at the other end. I willingly took the gamble, seeing it as an opportunity to repair our marriage.

Two years later, a high school chum, Trevor, invited me to be best man at his wedding, which was to take place in Alexandria, Louisiana. A quick map check affirmed that a road trip was appropriate. Rome, a major hub for the medical community in the tri-states, is tucked into the northwest corner of Georgia, far from interstates.

"You're on your own," my wife said. So I planned a solo exploration of the Deep South countryside. A road trip into virgin territory was an open invitation to explore. I loaded the Saab, kissed the baby, and off I went toward Alabama. Lakes, locks, rivers, levees, soybean, cotton fields, cotton fields, cotton fields. Mid-May, the fields had been planted and crops were growing. The terrain flattened out. The rural poverty and tenuous existences kept me rapt. Time melted.

About six that night, I breezed into Alexandria, navigated to the address given, and found that the wedding party had already left for dinner "out at the plantation." More directions, more navigating. I assumed that the "plantation" was a restaurant, but the longer I drove, the farther out into the country the road took me.

I finally arrived at what felt like "Tara" in *Gone with the Wind*: a two-story mansion, painted white on white, sitting in the middle of square miles of cotton fields. Several smaller outbuildings were set around the back and side of the main house. The first floor was elevated seven feet above the surrounding flat landscape. There were wide stairs coming off the wraparound porch fanning out onto the manicured lawn. Massive square columns supported the deep wraparound porch of full plank pine flooring and the tongue-and-groove pine beadboard ceiling. Inside, foot-deep crown molding accentuated the twelve-foot-high ceilings. Varnished heart pine floors glistened. The home looked like the day it was built, not restored. Time simply had passed it by. From the porch, no matter what direction I looked, all I could see were cotton fields.

The plantation survived the Civil War intact and remained in the family. The woman who originally owned it had tended to the wounds of a lieutenant in General William Tecumseh Sherman's Union Army. In gratitude, Sherman spared not only her house from the torch, but also her sister's house down the road. They were the only two homes still standing when the general and his troops marched out of Alexandria.

Dignified Black men in tuxedos and white gloves served mint juleps in their appropriate silver cups. My disquiet had just begun.

Not two months earlier, Los Angles had erupted in riots after a grand jury acquitted the four LAPD officers charged with beating Rodney King, an unarmed Black man stopped for DWI. L.A. was still smoldering while Black servants in tux and white gloves tended to my pleasure. But "Tara" wasn't a restaurant, and the servers weren't employed by a caterer. They were among a staff of ten to twelve Blacks who worked on the privately owned property.

The party moved inside for the sit-down dinner. The dining room held four round tables, each draped in white linen and set with ten place settings, finger bowls, and more silverware than I knew what to do with. The irony of servants swooshing around in tails and white gloves was unnerving.

The third high school chum, Ross, and I exchanged pensive glances, each wondering when the "massacre" would commence. Welcome to Alexandria, the place that emancipation had forgotten.

Ross and Trevor bunked at the house of his bride-to-be's great aunt, a self-appointed grand dame of ninety who still called all Blacks the "n" word. More discomfort. They put me up in the home of relatives who were out of town. I had the place to myself, along with a good selection of books. I settled in with *Winnie-the-Pooh*. There was enough down time to finish *The House at Pooh Corner* as well.

The next morning, Ross and I explored downtown and, that afternoon, played par-three golf with Trevor and other family members from both sides of the aisle.

The bride's father was an ex-congressman and a member of the Alexandria country club. Yet, for some reason, we had been sent off to a scruffy, grass-bereft, par-three course across town. Not all the way across the tracks, mind you, but definitely within a stone's throw from them.

We finished in time for a nap before the rehearsal dinner. The bride, an interior designer by education and trade, had invited two distinctly different groups of friends for the soiree. One, sorority sisters from Old Miss, her alma mater. True Southern Belles. The other, co-workers from a chic and trendy design studio in New York City. The studio owner had apprenticed under Andy Warhol and most, if not all who were invited, were gay or lesbian.

The sorority sisters arrived dressed as you would expect sorority sisters from the Deep South to, colorful floral dresses, tight bodices, full, fluffy skirts. All wore typed, stick-on nametags that read, "Should have been a bridesmaid," followed by their name."

Sandra, the bride, had limited her wedding party to two bridesmaids: her sister and her best friend. Trevor was stuck with Ross and me.

The New York crowd arrived dressed as you might expect a trendy, hip New York crowd to arrive at a trendy, hip New York nightclub. The two styles could not have contrasted more. Ross and I had front-row seats to watch the show. We could tell that this was shaping up to be a memorable event.

After toasts, speeches, and a really good meal, we became a happy, chummy group. The obligatory party over, we were off en masse to the only known gay bar in Alexandria. The sorority sisters had changed their clothes, which seemed to be liberating. We burst into a small drowsy, somewhat seedy bar/pool hall (five stools, one pool table) with a jukebox but no real dance floor.

The New York crowd greased the proprietor sufficiently to commandeer the jukebox and establish a quasi-dance floor. With the appropriate music selected, the real party was on. The locals had no idea what was happening, shrank against the walls, and stared incomprehensibly at the scene. Sorority sisters danced with the New Yorkers. New Yorkers danced with New Yorkers. Ross, Trevor, and I danced with everyone. By the end of the evening, the locals who were brave enough to stay had joined in.

Early that day, after finishing *Winnie-the-Pooh*, I reflected on my own marriage and decided it was irreparable and headed for the crapper. Strike two. Shortly after the revelation, someone introduced me to the bride's best friend, but only coincidentally, I'm sure. I made a serious attempt to impress her and danced my ass off. Later, I drove her back to her room, only to be politely rebuffed at the door. Probably for the best.

The next day, the wedding went off flawlessly. The reception was held at the country club. In retrospect, it was probably best that we were denied access to the grounds any earlier. Almost every family member thwarted my efforts to get next to the bride's friend. She was so fair, and I was so open to a new adventure.

After the long drive home, the marriage continued its downward spiral toward divorce. I was out by November. Within a year, we had signed the papers.

Old habits are slow to die.

Erato

Some find her draped in diamonds and Dior.
Others dance with her in clouds of drugs.
Still more see her through the blur of alcohol.
Without their muse,
they're barren, fruitless,
impotent to put pen to paper.

She comes to me
enshrouded in a Melancholia,
extinguishing my cheer,
yet igniting artistry from my soul:
no mere dysphoria,
immobilized, debilitated, aphasiac.

The more smothering her envelopment,
the more prolific my effusion,
transforming her dark veil
into my black verse.
Her sensuousness emblazes me,
and I am compelled to write.

I Shot My Cat

I shot my cat,
and that was that.
I didn't know he was my cat.
On his head sat a curious felt hat.
But there're no excuses.
I shot my cat,
and that was that.

I've pined so since he's passed
that one night a dream I cast
of him knocking at my front door,
standing a tallish six feet four,
wearing a deceptive chapeau
that befuddled me all the more.
Hand shaped, forefinger as the bore.

Digit aimed, rat-a-tat-tat,
I shot my cat,
a flurry of fur and a pile of scat.
Off he went; that was that.
If only I had known it was he . . .
Oh, such an egregious crime.
We could have had a grand old time.

Night Is Falling

Night is falling
and I need to find home.

I've been casting about
onto far-away shores,
resting my head
wherever she moors.

But now night is falling
and I need to find home.

Tempests tear at my soul
'til it's weary and battered.
As squalls rip memories,
my rigging is tattered.

Night is falling
and I need to find home.

I've reefed in the main
ever alone,
desperately needing
to find my way home.

Night is falling,
and I need to find home.

Perspective

For five or so years before I was born, my parents lived on a piece of land outside of Pittsburgh.

They had built a modest modern home strategically sited on the southern face of a hill, just below the crest. The south wall of the house was sixty feet long, twelve feet high, and solid glass. The eave overhung the glass wall by five feet, creating shade during the summer but allowing the sun to help warm our home during the winter. Hot water piped under the concrete floor provided the primary heat. The concrete—scored into four-foot squares and highly polished—looked like slate slabs. During the winter, I laid on that warm floor in front of those windows and looked out onto an eight-foot-wide natural stone patio that ran the length of the house.

My father sited the house with sufficient elevation so that with his careful tree culling—curated by my mother—we had an idyllic view. A steep bank planted with honeysuckle dropped down from the patio to a low stone wall that contained it. A lawn sloped a short distance to the edge of woods, which covered the rest of the valley and halfway up the opposing hill to the Smythe's house. Beyond lay a wheat field, a pine stand, and a far meadow that met the sky.

Indigenous wild cherry dominated these woods. The trees were tall and straight. Their big limbs competed for sunlight and burned best in our fireplace.

Our property stopped at the bottom of the valley, where a creek bisected the acreage, draining the two hills. From our patio, I couldn't see the Smythe's driveway snaking up the opposite slope, and trees obscured all but part of their first floor.

I would stand on the patio and think how far away their house looked. If I wanted to play with Kyle and Amanda, who were about my age, Mom or Dad would have to drive me two miles over winding country roads to get there.

One day, Kyle came up out of those woods with Amanda in tow, crossed the grass, climbed the stone stairs, cut through the honeysuckle, and stepped onto our patio, where he announced with great pride that he had "blazed a trail" through those woods connecting our two homes.

I often traversed that little path he made, down through those wild cherry trees, across the creek, back up the other side, past the broken-down barn, and up the last part of their driveway to their kitchen door. No more than a five-minute walk. That made their house feel not so far away and me a little bigger.

Beyond the Smythe's house, up a slight rise, lay the wheat field. The gold field made a stark contrast to that dark house. Even though the field was just behind their house, it looked twice as far away. Every year, I watched the farmer drive his combine harvester down one row and up the next. Stubble in the threshed field would change color from gold to light brown.

As I got older, my territory grew. We played hide-and-seek in the wheat field all summer and tobogganed down the gentle slopes all winter. At its far end grew the stand of pines. Their dark green marked a clear break from the gold field, adding another layer of color and mystery to the vista. But the pine stand also represented another goal. More growth, more courage. I set out on a great adventure to that pine barren. Through the well-worn paths of recently conquered territory, I approached the unknown.

The closer I got to the pines, the bigger they grew in size and depth. They were both inviting and foreboding. When I finally reached their boundary and peered in, I felt a long way from home. I stepped in a few feet. The massive pines almost immediately blocked out most of the sunlight, and the air was much cooler.

Needles blanketing the floor softened and deadened sound. The outside world receded to a whisper. I discovered that I wasn't as courageous as I thought—it felt scary. With each step, my surroundings grew darker, cooler, and quieter. Barely five minutes into my grand exploration, I turned around and high-tailed it home. When I reached the patio, I felt a little remorse for not having gone farther. I wondered about those pines. They didn't look quite as far away as before, but they were still mysterious.

The farthest I could see was the meadow. Light green grass that appeared to sit atop of those pines. I couldn't tell how far away the meadow was because the pine woods rolled down and out of sight before the meadow came up from behind them.

One day, when I was ten, I decided it was time to conquer the pines and reach the far meadow. Through the path in the wild cherry woods (which now held many memories of exploring, helping my dad cut down a tree or two, harvesting firewood for the winter, and strategically culling to perfect the view as directed by my mom); across the creek, where we hunted for crayfish and frogs; up past the broken-down barn, where I put a deep gash in the back of my head on a rusty nail that had stuck out from one of the beams (I bled all over the seat of the Smythe's car, and they had to get a new one, leaving a scar that much later in my life became skin cancer and had to be removed); past the Smythe's house, where Kyle took great delight in making me look and feel dumb (not a big challenge, as I was not very bright); across the wheat field, where we chased fireflies in the warm evenings; and into the foreboding pines. These conifers grew randomly and provided no clear way forward. I had to navigate through their chest-high, small, mostly dead limbs. It was so quiet that I made my way as stealthily as possible, as though I was trying to avoid waking something. It took a while, but I finally broke free of the pines and into the knee-high green grass of that far meadow. Soft, yet thick.

Halfway up a rolling hill, I looked back toward my house. It appeared small, but it didn't look miles away like I thought that it would. Yet, I had come a long way.

Not long thereafter, we moved away, and life moved on. New challenges presented themselves. When I would get stymied by something, I was always able to return to our patio, look out across that valley, and see that green meadow that touched the sky. I could look back at my home from that meadow and realize just how much farther I had come. The tougher the times, the more that view forward and backward brought me great solace and serenity.

All the memories forged in those woods—the hushed sounds, smells, coolness, changing seasons—a boy could not ask for better.

Reading

A page and a half to go,
my story
is all but written,
all characters
fully developed,
the outcome
all but certain,
plot twists exhausted,
my ink has run dry.
This author has
nothing left to say.

Well, maybe not.

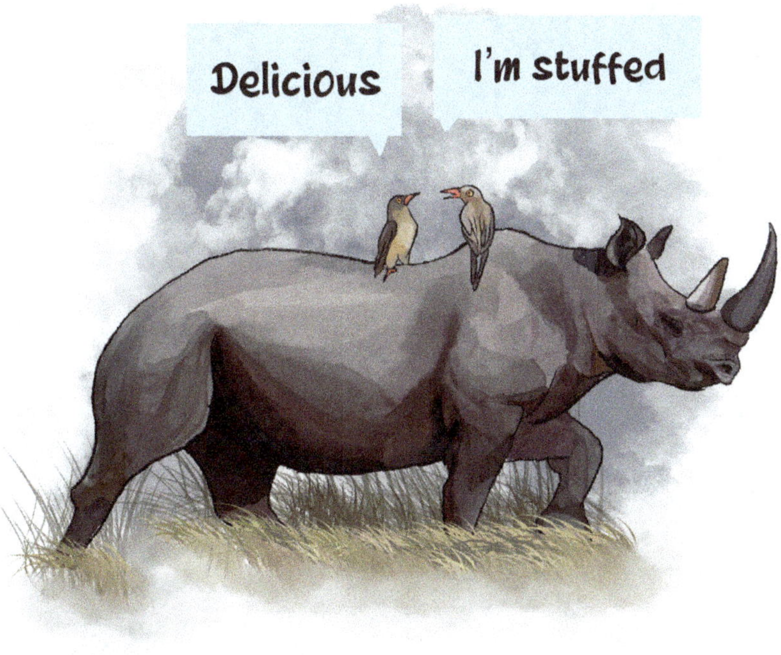
Delicious
I'm stuffed

www.ingramcontent.com/pod-product-compliance
Lightning Source LLC
Chambersburg PA
CBHW070706130626
46553CB00005B/1857